D0992025

The Dilemma
of Contemporary Theology

# The Dilemma
# of Contemporary Theology

*Prefigured in Luther, Pascal,*
*Kierkegaard, Nietzsche*

by
**PER LÖNNING**
Ph. D., Th. D.

**GREENWOOD PRESS, PUBLISHERS**
WESTPORT, CONNECTICUT

**Library of Congress Cataloging in Publication Data**

Lønning, Per.
The dilemma of contemporary theology prefigured
in Luther, Pascal, Kierkegaard, Nietzsche.

Reprint of the ed. published by Humanities Press,
New York, which was issued in series:
Scandinavian university books.
1.  Theology--Addresses, essays, lectures.
I.  Title.
[ BT15.L6  1978]        230        78-16470
ISBN 0-313-20596-5

Reprinted in 1978 by Greenwood Press, Inc.
51 Riverside Avenue, Westport, CT. 06880

Printed in the United States of America

10 9 8 7 6 5 4 3 2 1

# CONTENTS

# Preface

At first glance the present collection of theological essays —
most of them lectures on a variety of topics given at various
times and in various places — may seem a rather casual composition. What connection is there between Luther's hymnody,
Pascal's concept of cognition, different interpretations and
misinterpretations of Kierkegaard, the religious development of
Nietzsche, and an explicit problem deserving the label 'the
dilemma of contemporary theology'?

Let me give an answer as follows. The double lecture on
contemporary theology must be read as my own attempt at
summing up and giving expression to a theological puzzle which
for more than ten years has been, and still is, the basic incen-
tive behind my theological efforts. I started my postgraduate
work on Soeren Kierkegaard with the purpose of writing
a study on Christianity and existentialism, but soon got so
captivated by his dialectics that I got no further; I had to
complete my thesis on the Danish *Janus bifrons*. In the same
way my Pascal studies have been directed toward my own time;
but even they had to stop long before they had established a
formal link between past and present. But although it had not
been formally established or stated, to me personally the link
was there. My work with these two giants was, all the time,
a wrestling with 'the dilemma of contemporary theology'.
Much the same may be said of my preoccupation with Lutheran
hymnody and the life of Nietzsche, ancillary interests though
they have been. The 'historical' lectures chosen for the present

collection are included in order to exemplify and supplement the discussion of the 'contemporary' situation.

Except for the treatise of 'Kierkegaard's Paradox' (which was written for the Danish periodical *Orbis Litterarum* and printed in T.X, Fasc. 1-2, 1955 (in English)) all the essays in this book have actually been given as lectures, three at the Luther Theological Seminary, St Paul, Minn.; one at the University of Minnesota; one at Oslo University; and one in the literary society Athenaion, Oslo. Three of them have previously been published in Norwegian: the essay on Lutheran hymnody in *Tidsskrift for teologi og kirke* 1954, that on Nietzsche in *Kirke og Kultur* 1960 — in both cases with many notes and references which I have omitted in the present edition — and that on 'misunderstanding Soeren Kierkegaard' in my selection from Kierkegaard's works *Soeren Kierkegaard — et utvalg*, Oslo 1955.

Oslo, January 1961

*Per Lönning*

# I

## Conformitas Christi

*Conformitas Christi* — what do those words stand for? The
concept does not belong within our traditional scheme of *ordo
salutis* (the order of salvation). And it has not acted a decisive
part within the history of theology. In the course of the last
three or four decades, however, it has been turning up more
and more frequently in theological debate. As far as I can see,
this is more or less due to the modern Lutheran renaissance.
*Conformitas Christi* against *Imitatio Christi* — this has become
a very frequent description of the reformer's relation to Medieval piety.

No doubt modern theology has here grasped a central aspect
of Luther's thought. Even if the concept of 'conformity' has
a more than modest place in the life of the church throughout
the centuries, the matter itself has for some fifteen hundred
years been, so to speak, the very focus of theological effort.
It became the task of the first five centuries to answer the
question: who was Christ? And this answer was given so clearly
and impressively, that all succeeding generations have accepted
it as *the* Answer. Admitted that the terminology itself is that
of a distant epoch, admitted that 'natures' and 'substances'
and 'persons' are not the expressions we would have chosen
if it had been our task to formulate the creeds; the matter
itself, the deep intention behind the words, cannot be seriously
disputed — not by men who claim to be Christian believers.
But even if an answer was given to the question: who *was*
Christ — the central problem of Christianity is only solved

9

half-way. The remaining half is just as important, namely this: who *is* Christ? What does he mean to me today? What connection is there between Christ and my everyday life?

As far as I can see, this is the question which has occupied theology now for fifteen hundred years. And to this question the church has not been able to give an answer which could be commonly accepted. Here we find no *'quod semper, ubique et ab omnibus creditum est'* (what has been believed always, everywhere and by everybody). Here the roads simply divide and go in different directions.

My purpose here is not to give an historical survey of the problem and its development. Instead I would like the reader to take a look at the basic possible answers. After having located them, we should see how the answer *Conformitas Christi* is related to the rest of them, in order to find out if it could possibly help us toward a better solution than the more traditional and partly outworn concepts.

## 1.

To human beings today Christ is a rather remote person. We are divided from him by a gulf of nineteen hundred years. In addition to this he was, according to the sources, divided from his own time by a distance of one Eternity. Exactly speaking then, we should be divided from him by a distance of one Eternity, one thousand nine hundred and sixty years. This is quite a lot, that is, *if* we are going to base our entire hope of salvation upon him and his achievements *during his life on earth.*

The most convenient course for natural man in religious matters is always to stay undisturbed and alone in the company of Eternity, so he can just feel the resonance of it in his own breast and imagine he is running some nice little branch of Eternity himself. When some disturber of the peace gets in the way and cuts off his connections with Eternity, by claiming for example: 'I am the way, and the truth, and the life; no one cometh unto the Father but by me ...' — then the whole relation becomes complicated in a new and hitherto unknown way. First, this is an unbearable insult to natural man. It involves a frank proclamation that his private little branch of Eternity is neither more nor less than the workshop of a coiner, of a very unauthorized coiner. I do not have the least scrap of Eternity at my disposal. Secondly, if I accept the judgment, a new problem will arise, namely, How should I obtain the contact with Eternity which I am obviously lacking? How should I get in such a contact with him who calls himself the truth that I too might partake of this truth?

In order to survey the different answers, or rather the different ways of putting the same answer, in the Christian churches, let us start with the traditional psychological partition of the human spiritual faculties into three parts: will, feeling and thought. Different churches and different Christian movements have been disposed to emphasize these faculties in rather different ways, and to make now one, now another the dominant religious faculty. Let us see how.

We start by imagining with Henrik Ibsen that 'Det er viljen som det gjelder, viljen frigjør eller feller'. (It all depends upon the will, will sets free and will condemns.) What would a Christianity based upon such a maxim look like? I think we find the classical answer in the Medieval concept of *Imitatio Christi*, the imitation, or, as it has just as often been put, the following of Christ. Christ is, above all, the great model. All we have to do is to imitate him. If only we walk faithfully in his footsteps and always remember to ask ourselves 'What would Jesus have done in my place?' we are sure to reach the land of promise. Humility and poverty were, in the Middle Ages, considered the main expressions of this attitude. Generally they are not so strongly emphasized by those who take the same basic position today. When pursued with consistency and in earnest, the idea of imitation must, like every type of legalism, lead to one of two opposite results. Either the distress of Brand, the very same minister in the mouth of whom Ibsen put the famous words about the will: 'Never, never thou willst be like him, thou who in the flesh art born; try to serve him, try to strike him — anyhow thou art forlorn.' Or the self-contented pleasure of pharisaism: 'I thank Thee, my God, because I am not like other men, but, to state it quite frankly, like Thy beloved Son whom every day I successfully adopt as my model.'

Let us imagine the three faculties mentioned, but not as three points fully isolated from each other; instead let us suppose them to be three points situated on a circumference with a distance between them of approximately 120 degrees. This is to indicate that there is no definite borderline between psychological faculties; they just fade slowly into each other like colors in the spectrum. We now start to move along the arc of the circle from will and toward feeling. About halfway we meet with the Romantic conception, introduced by *Schleiermacher*, of Christ as an *Urbild* (archetype). This means: Christ is not a model who should be copied through decisions of the will. He is a kind of active and effective spiritual pattern. When we consider his magnificent picture, we are seized by his lofty and pure relation to God, so that we too are moved into this same relationship. Christ explores and reveals a new spiritual world, and all who are grasped by his overwhelming personal religious life are lifted into this brave new world. A beautiful thought, but it hardly corresponds to the Christian experience of fight with Satan, the world and the flesh. The *Urbild* theory makes Christianity an idyl, which is least of all what it is.

Relationship to Christ through feeling — there we stand at the gate of mysticism. Attention is exclusively concentrated upon Christ the present. The historical Jesus of Nazareth fades behind the 'bridegroom of the soul'. The mystic experience of Christ is often supposed to claim a considerable exercise of the will as its condition. Well known are the many Medieval descriptions of the mystical experience as a scale with many steps, with the rapture of divine unity as the supreme one. But the mounting of the scale may be a rather exhausting business which is not for beginners. The steps of this scale may, when considered separately, really serve a true and Christian sanctification. The qualification required for the beatific vision of God, is a radical mortification of all selfishness. *L'amour désinteressé* is the great aim.

But where is the connection between the historical Jesus and the 'bridegroom of the soul'? Consistently, mysticism and history must exclude each other. That means in the end that mysticism can give no real room to the historical deed of Christ. In Christian, as in all other kinds of mysticism, the distinction between the absolute obliteration of human self and the absolute exaltation of it can hardly be discerned. The distance between truth and untruth is not overcome, just overlooked.

Halfway between the Christianity of feeling and the Christianity of will we meet the Christianity of speculation. The soul embraces Christ through transforming him into some kind of idea. The concept of *logos* has, in the course of church history, been frequently misused for such a purpose. We might also mention the concept of God-Man as it occurs, for example, in the works of *Hegel*. To Hegel the unity of God and Man appears as a necessary link in the chain of a logical and cosmic process. By means of speculation the idea of God-Man reveals itself in human reason, and the act of incarnation completes itself through the philosophical mind. The resemblance to Schleiermacher's archetype-theology is obvious. But while the basic orientation in Schleiermacher is of a mystic-ethical kind, in Hegel it is definitely mystic-metaphysical. Thus Hegel makes himself guilty, not only of establishing a false harmony between God and man, but also of doing away completely with the historical figure of Christ. His Christ comes seemingly close to contemporary man, no doubt, but this Christ has little, if anything, to do with the man Jesus of Nazareth. This idea of God-Man might have been conceived and exploited by some human brain without the least contact with a message of real, historical events.

We proceed along the circular arc; and soon we find a place for orthodoxy. Even that tries to grasp Christ by means of reason, but in a rather different way. It is not the person of Christ that it tries to grasp — its profound Christian instinct makes it recoil with horror from every, or almost every attempt to rationalize the paradox of incarnation. What it rationalizes are the achievements of Christ. And that is perhaps no better. *Anselm's* doctrine of atonement and the post-Melanchthonian doctrine of justification with their strictly juridical considerations leave no real room for the living Christ, only for a Christ who *has* lived. Certainly, the orthodox tradition does point to the living present Lord in other paragraphs, but isn't it really too bad when a theological system places a Christ of the past in one paragraph and a Christ of the present in another, with no real organic connection between them? Through the concept of 'imputation' the merits of Christ are transferred to us; we have come to be possessors of an account in the Universal Celestial Bank. But where is the basic fellowship with Christ, where is the strictly personal relationship? Even if a doctrine of *unio mystica* is by no means lacking in the orthodox system, it is not really related with the basic concepts of faith and justification.

To make our circle complete, we come again toward our starting point: the Christianity of will. As a stage between the intellectualistic and the moralistic conceptions we may place the theology of the Enlightenment. According to this theology Christ is conceived as the great teacher of mankind. The thing connecting us with him is his noble and exalted teaching of ethics. The point is to become informed by Jesus and, on the basis of his new and purified concepts of religion, to lead a life in 'virtue' and blissful complacency. I don't think that any of my readers would feel a need for a formal refutation of this paramount mixture of the weak sides of moralism and intellectualism.

We have made our tour of the circle. We have come upon the piety of imitation, the theology of archetypology, mysticism, speculation, orthodoxism and enlightenment. If we had continued we might have made the same tour once or twice more — but I should definitely not care to perpetuate the journey. The circle described is, in fact, what we might call the *circle of immanence*. Along its circumference we could, indeed, place all the possible attempts man has made to bridge the gulf between Christ and himself. Multifarious are his possibilities, but in their essence they are pretty much alike. The decisive fact in them all is that the Biblical message of Christ present, emphatic and realistic as it is, has not been justly

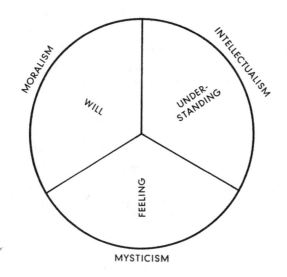

rendered. The person of Christ himself is absent, and the salvatory presence is that of his doctrine, his example or his merit. Or he is made present by abstracting from his historical appearance, his suffering, his death and resurrection — all this is left behind as belonging to some remote past — and behold, the presence which comes out of this is not the presence of Christ either.

## 2.

According to the Bible, Christ is present exactly in the quality of crucified and resurrected; indeed his death and resurrection are in some sense being effected in his church here and now. Certainly, 'It is finished'; Christ has brought about an eternal redemption which needs no repetition and no supplement. But 'finished' in this connection means least of all 'past'. There is something paradoxical in the Christian concept of history. Some years ago the famous Swiss professor *Oscar Cullmann* wrote a treatise on *Christus und die Zeit* (Christ and Time), where he strongly advocates that Christianity presupposes a linear concept of time. It seems to me that Professor Cullmann in his argumentation overlooks a good

15

deal of the New Testament material. Cullmann holds the old theological idea of a *Heilsgeschichte* (salvatory history) according to which every Biblical event is conceived as a point which will, in the next moment, be outdistanced by another point. Consequently, there exists no real contemporaneousness with the Cross and with the resurrection of Christ. They are finished events belonging to the past, and we are called to react upon them from afar. Cullmann is, of course, basically right in emphasizing the historic character of the deed of redemption and the *consummatum* of the atonement as well. But besides these good intentions he shows an astonishing one-sidedness, which falls completely short of the Biblical reality σὺν χριστῷ (with Christ).

Having mentioned this term, we stand at the very source of the Conformitas motif. The word itself, *conformitas,* or, as it would be in Greek, συμμόρφωσις, does not occur in the New Testament. However, we meet its root in verbal form in Phil. iii:10, and as an adjective in Rom. viii:29 and Phil. iii:21. We shall soon come back to these references. An idea of *conformitas* seems, furthermore, to be the basis of the frequently repeated formula σὺν χριστῷ and of many of the notions connected with the prefix σύν; for example, συμπάσχειν, suffer together with; συναποθνῄσκειν, die together with; συσταυροῦσθαι, be crucified together with; σύμφυτος, grown together with; συζῆν, live together with; συζωοποιεῖν, bring to life together with; συνεγείρειν, wake up together with; συνδοξάζεσθαι, be glorified together with; and συμβασιλεύειν, rule together with.

As will already be clear from this enumeration, the New Testament idea of *Conformitas* is essentially related to the cycles: death/resurrection and abasement/exaltation. The road Christ had to walk through destruction to life is thought to be a reality actually present, the believer being led along the same road σὺν χριστῷ. This by no means implies that the historical facts in themselves become a matter of indifference. When the death and resurrection of Christ can be significant events today, it is exactly because they have really happened. But this *having happened* is just not the complete truth.

Let us take a closer look at some details of New Testament

preaching. In Phil. iii:10 we find, as already mentioned, the verb συμμορφίζεσθαι. It occurs in the well-known passage where Paul speaks of his blameless righteousness, according to the law, which, however, he has counted as dirt in order to win another and better righteousness, namely through faith in Christ. And so he goes on: '. . . that I may know him, and the power of his resurrection, and the fellowship of his sufferings, becoming *conformed* unto his death; if by any means I may attain unto the resurrection from the dead.' At first glance 'the power of his resurrection' and 'the fellowship of his sufferings' do not necessarily indicate a real presence of the historical events themselves. Even 'becoming conformed unto his death' might be interpreted simply as supposing his death to exercise some kind of a causal influence throughout the centuries, either as an example of humility or as some kind of *Urbild* affecting our emotional life. However, a series of other passages in the Pauline letters indicate that something distinctively more must be meant. In Col. ii:20 the author states that 'ye died with Christ from the rudiments of this world', and further: 'ye were raised together with Christ . . . ye died, and your life is hid with Christ in God . . . When Christ, who is our life, shall be manifested, then ye shall also be manifested with him in glory'. And Gal. ii:20: 'I have been crucified with Christ, and it is no longer I that live but Christ liveth in me . . .'

Just as Christ passed from death unto life, the triumphant certainty expresses itself over and over again: if we die together with Christ, we are also going to live together with him. 'If we suffer together with him, we shall also reign together with him.' Read, for instance, the glorious interpretation of this truth in the passage of the treasure in earthen vessels, 2 Cor. ii:7-14!

A rather peculiar circumstance is that our resurrection with Christ is sometimes spoken of as a past, sometimes as a future event. We have pointed out some examples of the 'futuristic' expression. In Eph. ii and Col. ii we find the resurrection of the Christian described as something already having taken place. The Ephesian passage speaks of God's great work of mercy toward us who were formerly dead in our sins and trespasses. Here we see that the death a Christian is delivered from is conceived somewhat differently from the way it is in the passages already quoted. There we met the idea that the sinner has to pass through a death and a resurrection together with Christ. Here we meet with the presupposition that man in himself *is* dead, and the task of Christ is in this connection exclusively understood as lifegiving. 'God, being rich in mercy ... even when we were dead through our trespasses, quickened us together with Christ ... and raised us up with him, and made us to sit with him in heavenly places, in Christ Jesus ...' (Eph. ii:4-6.) In Col. the concept is exactly the same: 'You being dead through your trespasses and the uncircumcision of your flesh, you, I say, did he quicken together with him, having forgiven us all our trespasses.' Then the question at once will arise: when did this resurrection with Christ take place? At the moment Christ rose again, or at the moment the individual believer was incorporated into the Christian community? I think that the application of an absolute either-or will not be appropriate in this setting. In Eph. iv we meet the concept that Christ on his journey from hell to heaven 'led captivity captive'. And certainly, among the captives he carried off from prison were ourselves. The meaning of this passage is not, as has so frequently and mistakenly been believed in the history of the church, some mythological theory of the pious men of the old covenant being delivered from their preliminary custody in a subterranean prison. The point is, as may be plainly seen when the passage is read in its context, that all those who adhere to Christ throughout all the centuries were carried out of damnation through his resurrection. The usual Pauline way of referring to this fact, however, is not to place the individual believer within the finished accomplishment of Christ, but to place this accomplishment within present everyday life. His usual way is not to make us contemporaries of Christ, but to make Christ a contemporary of ours. We were not present at Calvary, but Calvary is present here among us.

The Holy history, that is, the life of Christ, *Soeren Kierkegaard* argues, stands alone by itself outside history. It follows every new generation with an eternal contemporaneousness. This statement, it seems to me, does full justice to the words of St. Paul.

What we have stated is this: the New Testament idea of *conformitas* does not make a compact, logical entity. The emphasis is sometimes laid upon the past tense: our resurrection (in some connections, our death and resurrection) with Christ is something completed some 1900 years ago; sometimes upon the present: Christian life is an ever-renewed dying and rising again with Christ; sometimes upon the future: having already partaken of the death of Christ, we can look forward to partaking also of his resurrection.

Yet, however this may be, there is a basic motive common to the diverging expressions. Although they are real events having taken place once for all, the death, the resurrection and the ascension of Christ get their full meaning in his Church as he, present in person, takes men into community with his sufferings and his triumph. We have shown this from the letters of Paul, but it is easy to see how the idea corresponds with the Johannine teaching of the Savior as the Way, the Truth and the Life. Here too salvation means the personal presence of Christ, in whom the believer is really being embodied. Neither the historical fact of the redemption nor the future fulfillment is being questioned. John is not a mystic placing all the emphasis on the sweet communion of present *unio mystica*, as he has so frequently been portrayed. The Christian life is clearly described, though, as fellowship with the ever-present Christ, a fellowship through which eternal life is constantly being communicated to the believer. The living water, the bread of life, the vine which the branches share in — all these are unmistakable expressions of the basic importance of personal fellowship with the Lord today. The very idea of *conformitas* is not so sharply pointed out as in the Pauline writings, and this seems due to the fact that while John gives broader attention to the importance of incarnation for our fellowship with Christ, Paul emphasizes the cross and the resurrection — a difference in emphasis which by no means implies contradiction in matter.

19

The question we will have to face next is this: how does man enter into the *conformitas Christi*? Or perhaps we had better ask: how can we, in giving account of this *conformitas*, avoid plunging into one of the errors we have revealed along the mighty circumference of immanence? How can we escape mysticism, moralism and intellectualism and any kind of mixture between them by way of *conformitas*? It should be obvious that from the viewpoint of religious psychology all the errors listed bear in themselves an element of real truth. Their essential fault is not so much what they say as what they omit. Their error rests in their claim of exclusiveness. No straightforward logical statement can give us the fullness of Christ (not even the fullness of a human person for that matter). What we really need is not an unequivocal theory of Christian psychology, but a concept of Christ which leaves the entire spectrum of psychological possibilities at their worth and stretches out beyond them to make the living Christ the real focus of Christian self-understanding.

To illustrate what I mean, I propose that we add to our circle a point placed outside it and above its level. Let us imagine this point connected with the circumference by an infinity of lines corresponding to any point along the circumference. We have drawn a cone. Let us imagine the idea of the entire solid. Human logic moves in the simple plane. But the three dimensions of a solid cannot be essentially reproduced in the two dimensions of the plane. You can draw a cone on a sheet of paper, but the drawing itself is not a cone like the drawing of a circle is a real circle. The drawing can in some way represent the cone to me, it can give me the suggestions which I need in order to depict what a person tries to communicate to me on the subject of cones. But it is in itself by no means a cone. Just as the paper is incapable of catching solids, so thought is helpless at catching the human 'I' and at grasping personal relationships. It can grasp a moral paradigm, it can grasp a program of mystical performances, it can grasp an account of credits and debits. But it just cannot grasp the communion

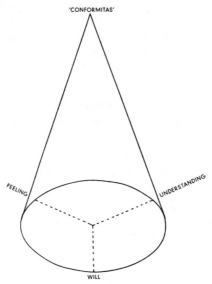

'CONFORMITAS'

FEELING

UNDERSTANDING

WILL

of a human 'I' and a human 'Thou'. And even less the communion with a man who, besides being a man, is the Son of God. Theology can only represent this relation to us as the paper can represent a solid. It gives suggestions which are valid only so far as they succeed in actualizing a knowledge which theology, itself, has not been able to convey.

That the death and resurrection of Christ should be events really present cannot at all be apprehended by logic. An event as such is not transferable from one time to another. Its effects, its meaning, its appeal, and so on, are in some respects conveyable, but not the event itself.

It should thus become clear that *conformitas Christi* cannot be secured by some kind of logical definition or by some well defined psychological quality. No program and no recipe is synonymous with the presence of Christ. When *Luther* argues that *in ipsa fide Christus adest,* this is not in contradiction to what I have maintained; for how could faith be identified with one or the other psychological quality?

There exists, humanly speaking, no guarantee of the presence of Christ. Just a promise, supported by visible signs which he who has given the promise, himself has chosen. 'Or are you

21

ignorant that all we who were baptized into Christ Jesus were baptized into his death? We were buried therefore with him through baptism into the death; that like as Christ was raised from the dead through the glory of the Father, so we also might walk in the newness of life. For if we have become united with him by the likeness of his death, we shall be also by the likeness of his resurrection . . .' (Rom. vi:3-5) Also the presence of Christ in Holy Communion is closely related to his death and resurrection. Remember the very circumstances of its institution. As far as I know, there is likewise a widespread agreement among the exegetes of our time that the record of the blood and water pouring out of the Lord's side (John xix:34) is meant to indicate how the sacraments proceed from his death.

The Roman concept of the mass sacrifice contains quite a profound element of truth. It is only a pity that evangelical theology has been staring so intensely at the obvious errors of the same doctrine that it has thrown out the baby with the bath water. It is true that Holy Communion is in some sense a repetition of what happened at Golgotha, and, we add, of what happened when the grave was broken. The word 'repetition', however, is perhaps not in itself very appropriate. It does not render justice to the words, 'It is finished'. It may be taken as suggesting a 'once-more' which is just meaningless. The most appropriate notion might be that of *conformitas*. The major error of the Roman Church is not the idea of the sacrifice of Christ present in Holy Communion, but, firstly, the concept of this sacrifice in itself, namely, as in the category of 'merits'; secondly, the concept of church and priesthood which stresses God's action *through* the church at the cost of his action *with* the church; and, thirdly, the isolation of the consecration from the Lord's Supper, which makes the presence of Christ a static matter: he is present in the elements apart from their being received by a congregation of communicants. The reservation and adoration of the elements exclude a right understanding of the real *conformitas*, which is an event taking place *with* us, not an accomplished matter the hierarchy can place *before* us.

Through the preaching of the Word, and through Baptism

and Holy Communion, men are being integrated into the body of Christ. The death and resurrection in baptism is the introduction to a life in daily death and resurrection, which is again a prolegomenon to the last and definitive death and resurrection. Life in the church is a life in Christ, life tending toward God's great aim. 'For whom he foreknew, he also foreordained to be conformed (σύμμορφοι) to the image of his son.' Death and resurrection, that is also what Luther expresses in his well-known formulation *simul justus et peccator*. A point which is clearly expressed in a passage we have already quoted from Col. iii:3: 'Ye died, and your life is hidden with Christ in God.' That means: your communion with Christ is present only insofar as it is striving to come into presence, your life is a permanent dying, Christ is here in his suffering and debasement, unrecognizable to human eyes, given up to death — and my life consists in going through all this with him. 'When Christ, our life, shall be manifested, then shall ye also be manifested, with him in glory.' That means: the incessant to and fro of death and resurrection will cease. Life will be triumphant, resurrection alone remains. We are no more 'bearing about in the body the dying of Jesus' (2. Cor. iv:20), but just his living.

*Conformitas Christi* can in no way be treated as some kind of a dogmatic locus. Nor does it claim to be the only legitimate aspect of Christian life. Juridical, ethical, mystical — or whatever — considerations may also be in their right; their limited right. But the right of the *conformitas*-motif cannot be subject to limitations. It is the top point of the cone, and should therefore be treated as superior to all other christological and soteriological deliberations. The paradoxical unity of 'it is finished' and 'it is being finished', of Christ given for us and of us incorporated in Christ, together with its clear eschatological outlook gives expression to the fullness ˴f basic Christian concerns. Justification and mystical communion, which have so often been put beside each other without any real connection, or even put up against each other as mortal enemies, are here clearly revealed as complementary expressions of the same concern. Perhaps this is the reason why Christian hymn writers

23

have always been more clever at expressing it than Christian theologians.

To demonstrate this, just let me quote from two hymns which exactly emphasize what I have been trying to say. I start with a Swedish hymn from our own century, written by the late Bishop J. A. Eklund. ('Med Jesus fram i de bästa åren . . .')

With Jesus forth when the call is ringing
The Spirit's speaking a joyful day.
And in temptation, when he is bringing
You out in deserts where weak you'll stay
And start the strife, an incessant strife,
Which strips of peace your entire life.

With Jesus forth to proclaim his favor,
The happy message of blissful gain.
With Jesus up on the heights of Tabor
Where beams of glory do still remain.
With Jesus down in the valley deep,
To still the pains of the ones who weep.

With Jesus forth in the last affliction,
Your life his Father to sacrifice.
With Jesus forth in the same direction:
A cross erected by human vice.
Forth to the seal of a closed grave,
With this inscription: his life he gave.

With Jesus forth from the broken fetter
Which held all life in a mortal night.
With Jesus forth to a morning better
Revivified for a dawning bright.
With Jesus forth to the heav'nly height
Where God is sun and the Lamb is light.

Or as Paulus Gerhardt proclaims in his matchless Easter hymn *Auf, auf, mein Herz mit Freuden*, where, after having pictured the darkness at the grave and then the Savior, so to say, leaping forth from it in the dawn of morning, swinging his standard and shouting 'Victory!', he goes on:

24

Das ist mir anzuschauen  
Ein rechtes Freudenspiel.  
Nun soll mir nicht mehr grauen  
Vor allem was mir will  
Entnehmen meinen Mut  
Zusamt dem edlen Gut  
So mir durch Jesum Christ  
Aus Lieb erworben ist.

This is a sight that gladdens;  
What peace it does impart!  
Now nothing ever saddens  
The joy within my heart.  
No gloom shall ever shake,  
No foe shall ever take,  
The hope which God's own son  
In love for me has won.

Die Höll und ihre Rotten,  
Die krümmen mir kein Haar.  
Der Sünden kann ich spotten,  
Bleib allzeit ohn Gefahr.  
Der Tod mit seiner Macht  
Wird nichts bei mir geacht:  
Er bleibt ein totes Bild,  
Und wär er noch so wild.

Now hell, its prince, the devil,  
Of all their pow'r are shorn.  
Now I am safe from evil,  
And sin I laugh to scorn.  
Grim death with all its might,  
Cannot my soul afright;  
He is a pow'rless form,  
Howe'er he rave and storm.

Die Welt ist mir ein Lachen  
Mit ihrem grossen Zorn.  
Sie zürnt und kann nichts machen,  
All Arbeit ist verlorn.  
Die Trübsal trübt mir nicht  
Mein Herz und Angesicht,  
Das Unglück ist mein Glück,  
Die Nacht mein Sonnenblick.

The world against me rageth,  
Its fury I disdain.  
Though bitter war it wageth,  
Its work is all in vain.  
My heart from care is free,  
No trouble troubles me.  
Misfortune now is play,  
And night is bright as day.

Because:

Ich hang und bleib auch hangen  
An Christo als ein Glied;  
Wo mein Haupt durch is gangen,  
Da nimmt er mich auch mit.  
Er reisset durch den Tod,  
Durch Welt, durch Sünd, durch Not,  
Er reisset durch die Höll,  
Ich bin stets sein Gesell.

Now I will cling forever  
To Christ, my Savior true;  
My Lord will leave me never,  
Whate'er he passeth through.  
He rends death's iron chain,  
He breaks through sin and pain,  
He shatters hell's dark thrall,  
I follow him through all.

Er dringt zum Saal der Ehren,  
Ich folg ihm immer nach  
Und darf mich gar nicht kehren  
An einzig Ungemach.  
Es tobe, was da kann,  
Mein Haupt nimmt sich mein an,  
Mein Heiland ist mein Schild,  
Der alles Toben stillt.

To halls of heavenly splendor  
With him I penetrate;  
And trouble ne'er may hinder  
Nor make me hesitate.  
Let tempest rage at will,  
My Savior shields me still;  
He grants abiding peace  
And bids all tumult cease.

| | |
|---|---|
| Er bringt mich and die Pforten, | He brings me to the portal |
| Die in den Himmel führt, | That leads to bliss untold, |
| Daran mit güldnen Worten | Whereon the rime immortal |
| Der Reim gelesen wird: | Is found in script of gold: |
| Wer dort wird mit verhöhnt, | Who there my cross hath shared |
| Wird hier auch mit gekröhnt; | Finds here a crown prepared; |
| Wer dort mit Sterben geht, | Who there with me hath died |
| Wird hier auch mit erhöht. | Shall here be glorified. |

(The English translation by John Kelly (1867) involves a considerable weakening of the *conformitas-motif*. Notice the loss of the concept of the Body of Christ, likewise the loss of at least two 'mit'-s in the last verse.)

# II

## Luther and his 'Successors' —
## Revealed in their Hymnody

Research done in the history of theology, it seems to me, has to an amazing degree eschewed that adjustment of its conclusions which must have resulted, had it faced up to a thorough theological analysis of hymns and devotional literature. The purpose of this essay is to sketch the outline of theological development in the time between the Reformation and Pietism, as it may be studied in the work of some of the most outstanding hymn writers of the period. Attention to the topic of 'Communion with Christ', will, I think, make particularly apparent the change in theological emphasis which took place during the sixteenth and the seventeenth centuries.

In his interesting study of *Barock und Aufklärung im geistlichen Lied* (1951), *Kurt Berger* makes an attempt to trace the development as follows: the intensive exertions of the Baroque (orthodoxism) to reconcile the soul, the world and God are alleviated by the *Jesus-Liebe* of Pietism and gradually changed into the harmonious religious feeling of the Enlightenment. The dark thunder-God of Orthodoxism, the 'God of grimness and grace', must, by and by, yield place to the clement 'God Father' — a change which to Berger means a real comeback of the Reformation. Furthermore his orientation is not determined by taking Luther as the starting point of the development, but by taking Goethe as its end. Luther is just a single swallow predicting a summer which still lies far ahead.

This concept will, I think, be shown to be untenable in view of the facts to which I shall call attention in the following. To indicate the direction of the argument, it may be useful to start with a brief summing up of my conclusions. Theologically, the development of hymn writing from Luther up to the Enlightenment is a very coherent process. The presence of Christ to the faithful means two entirely different things in the hymns of Luther and in those of clear-cut Pietism and of its heir, Enlightenment. As early as in the latter half of the seventeenth century the change from one to the other seems fully accomplished. The eighteenth century brings essentially no more and no less than a clarification and a systematization of tendencies which already in the late seventeenth century had effectively broken through in every area of church life.

We are now going to look at the idea of communion with Christ, first as it is found in the hymns of *Martin Luther*, then as manifested in three of the most popular hymn writers of the late seventeenth century: *Angelus Silesius, Heinrich Müller* and *Ahasverus Fritsch*. Finally, to get an impression of how the change took place, we shall take a look at three of the poets who come, chronologically and thematically, between the beginning and the end of this change, *Johann Walter, Johann Heermann* and *Paulus Gerhardt*.

## 1.

We need few words to describe what communion with Christ means in Luther's own hymns. His song is dedicated to the unique champion, the man of contrast and conflict, God's eternal and almighty Son, born poor and unhonored into this world, but come expressly to bring about a contrary transformation in the condition of man. Christ has made himself one with all poor and perished people and made them one with him in eternal glory. The great contrast in Christ, the contrast between his eternal identity and the fate he chooses to suffer in this world, is the prototype of the contrast in which the faithful also have to live, namely, a contrast between the eternal richness bestowed upon them by grace and received by them in faith, and the visible and undisputable poverty which is the

28

only personal property of sinful men. Communion with Christ is a communion of faith; the glory of Christ was hidden in this world, and so is the glorious communion with him; it escapes every kind of introspection and psychological analysis. I have to take his word for it and believe it, that is all. Communion with Christ thus means struggle and affliction, but in the midst of all this, Christ himself, with divine powers, sustains our weakness.

Er sprach zu mir «halt dich an
                                mich,
Es soll dir ytzt gelingen,
Ich geb mich selber gantz für dich,
Da will ich fur dich ringen.
Den ich byn deyn und du byst meyn,
Und wo ich bleib, da soltu seyn,
Unns soll der feind nich scheyden.

To me He spake: Hold fast to Me,
I am thy Rock and Castle;
Thy Ransom I Myself will be,
For thee I strive and wrestle;
For I am with thee, I am thine,
And evermore thou shalt be Mine;
The foe shall not divide us.

Vergiessen wird er mir meyn blut,
Dazu mein leben rawben:
Da leyde ich alles dir zu gutt,
Da halt mit festem glauben:
Den todt verschlingt dz leben meyn,
Meyn unschult tregt die sunden
                                deyn,
Da bistu selig worden.»

The Foe shall shed my Precious
                                blood,
Me of My life bereaving.
All this I suffer for thy good;
Be steadfast and believing.
Life shall from death the victory
                                win,
My innocence shall bear thy sin;
So art thou blest forever.

Der sohn des vatters, Gott von ard,
Eyn gast yn der werlet ward,
Unnd furt uns aus dem yamer tall,
Er macht uns erben yn seym saal.

Though Son of God, by Angels
                                blessed,
To our world he came as guest,
And brings us from afflictions all
To glory great in Heaven's hall.

Er yst auff erden kommen arm,
Das er unser sych erbarm
Und ynn dem hymel machet reich
Und seynen lieben Engeln gleich.

He came to us in darksome night,
To make us children of the light,
To give the poor a fate divine:
In richness like his Angels shine.

Neither of the two hymns we have quoted from, *Nun freut euch liebe Christen g'mein* and *Gelobet seist du, Jesu Christ* is, like many of his other hymns, an adaptation of a Psalm or of some particular Ancient or Medieval hymn. But even in these compositions of his own, we sense Luther's predilection for the motifs of ancient hymnody. As we see from his translations, 'Ambrosian' hymns are adopted into his own thought and experience without the least effort of adaptation. For just two examples, from *Veni redemptor gentium* take these stanzas:

| | |
|---|---|
| Der du bist dem vater gleich, | Thou who aye with God art one, |
| Fur hynaus den sieg ym fleisch, | In our flesh the vict'ry won, |
| Das dein ewig gots gewalt | That Thy great, eternal gain |
| Ynn unns das kranck fleysch | Might our feeble flesh sustain. |
| enthallt. | |

Aequalis æterno patri
Carnis tropæo accingere.
Infirma nostri corporis
Virtute firmans perpetim.

| | |
|---|---|
| Der selig schepffer aller ding | The blessed Maker of us all |
| Zoch an ein knechtes leib gering, | Dressed in the body of a thrall |
| Das er das fleisch durch fleisch erworb | By flesh to conquer our flesh, |
| Und sein geschepff nicht als verdorb. | Lest His creation should perish. |

Beatus auctor seculi
Servile corpus induit.
Ut carne carnem liberans
Ne perderet quod condidit.

We find only one stanza in the entire hymnody of Luther that seems to depart from this theological pattern, namely, one belonging to *Vom Himmel hoch, da komm' ich her*, presented by Luther himself as 'A children's Christmas carol'. Yet even here the theme is the richness and the poverty of Christ and their significance for faith. But, suddenly, another theme seems to prevail:

| | |
|---|---|
| Ah, mein herzliebes Ihesulin, | O, dear beloved little Christ, |
| Mach dir ein rein sanfft bettelin, | Come, choose Thy cradle in my |
| Zu rugen in mein herzens schrein, | breast. |
| Das ich nimer vergesse dein. | Shrine for Thy rest my heart let be, |
| | That aye I might remember Thee. |

The transition to this from the preceding verses consists not only in a change of images and expressions, but at the same time in a transition from predication to adoration. Certainly, the expressions here come closer to Medieval mysticism than to the incarnation theology of the Ancient church. Is not Luther here really speaking of a harmonious emotional inhabitation of Christ in the pious soul? Probably its place within the totality of the hymn, as well as the consciously infantile mode of expression used throughout the *Lied,* should indicate that the stanza ought not to be twisted in the hands of over-zealous dogmaticians. A static *fruitio Christi* is not at all the point. It is just gratitude for God's having made himself like the sinner in order to make the sinner like God, which here bursts out in joyous praise. The heart opens itself to the Christ-Kind, not in order to gain some particular blessing in return, but in thanks for a blessing already received. The adoration becomes the natural expression of thanksgiving; and that, in this wonderful Christmas carol, is the decisive point. And exactly at this point the religious poetry of the following age departs from the Reformer's pattern.

## 2.

Let us observe the contrast. We can choose to start with *Angelus Silesius* (Johann Scheffler, 1624-77) even though most of his religious poetry dates from the period after his conversion to the Roman church, for Scheffler's basic concept of Christianity seems to have been fixed long before he nominally left the Lutheran church. His subsequent attempts to fence his mysticism into the sacramental frame of Roman Catholicism are not always convincing. In addition to this his poetry has definitely exercised by far its largest influence among Protestants. Even today his position within Protestant hymnals testifies to this. 'Thee will I love till the pure fire / Fills my whole soul with chaste desire' — echoes even in the new American Lutheran Hymnal (1958). In the most orthodox Lutheran hymnal in America, that of the late Synodical Conference, the 'chaste desire' has disappeared, and the sentence is moderated to; 'Thee will I love, O light Divine, So long as life is mine'.

Even in Scheffler's poetry we find some consciousness of the forgiveness of sin as an integral part of Christian Life. But it cannot be claimed that this is a theme which seriously engages his poetic talent. The most obvious trend in his poems is the quest for spiritual *Wohl-lust*. When he depicts religious communion the terms he chooses are predominantly erotic ones. Or he may use expressions like, '*Lass meine Seel' ein Bienelein / Auf deinen Rosen-Wunden sein.*' (Oh, let my soul be a little bee on Thy rosy wounds!)

| | |
|---|---|
| Ach dass ich doch nur möchte seyn | O, might there always be in me |
| Gleich wie ein kluges Bienelein! | The wisdom of a little bee |
| Sie wolt' ich mich erheben: | To imitate her action. |
| Ich hinge mich an seine Brust | Then I would cling close to His |
| Und bliebe da nach Wuntsch und | breast, |
| Lust | And stay according to my lust, |
| Biss ich zerfliesse, kleben. | Till merged in satisfaction. |

The world is void and blissless, and human desire for happiness must seek its object somewhere else:

| | |
|---|---|
| Keine Lust ist auff der Welt, | In this world no lust at all |
| Die mein Hertz zu frieden stellt; | Can my heart enjoyment call. |
| Dein, O Jesu, bey mir seyn | Jesus, when Thou art my own, |
| Nenn ich meine Lust allein. | Thee I call my lust alone. |

Therefore the poet cries to Jesus: 'Hurry to come and make me partaker of the rapture of eternal love!' A prayer which, of course, should not be given an eschatological but a purely psychological exegesis. It is the joyful feeling of the presence of the bridegroom which the soul is here invoking.

| | |
|---|---|
| Drumb so komm doch bald zu mir | Therefore, hurry now to me, |
| Und erfreue mich mit dir; | Entertain my soul with Thee; |
| Schleuss mich in die Armen ein, | Hug me in Thy arms that were |
| Die für mich verwundet seyn. | Wounded once for me, my dear. |

Reich mir deinen süssen Mund.
Thu mir deine Liebe kund;
Druck mich an die zarte Brust.
Die mir ewig schaffet Lust.

Lass mich in den Armen
Deiner Huld erwarmen:
Lass mich dich genissen
Und in deinem Lichte,
Schönstes Angesichte,
Deine Lippen küssen.

Deine Liebes-Küsse
Sind für Zukker-süsse;
Dein Geruch ist gänzlich gleich
Gott und seinem Himmelreich.

I'll enjoy Thy mouth so sweet,
Let me know Thy loving heat.
Hug me to Thy clement breast,
Which forever is my lust.

In Thy arms embrace me,
Warm me there and grace me:
Let me taste Thy blisses,
And in glory streaming,
Countenance most beaming,
Touch Thy lips with kisses.

Every kiss caressing,
Sweet like sugar blessing,
Thy aroma gently fit:
God and Heaven are in it.

It is obvious that the experience of the presence of Christ expressed in stanzas like these has no connection whatsoever with the belief that the poverty and humility of Christ corresponds to the burden of my sins, which he has undertaken to bear, and that Christian happiness arises from belief in his richness and glory as it has been promised to me by the Gospel. The point to Scheffler is the emotional experience taking place in his own soul. In the communion of sweet love the barrier between Christ and ourselves is wiped out perceptibly and sensuously.

Die betrübte Seele
Jauchzt in ihrer Höle,
Denn du tränkst sie wie ein Strom,
Macht sie heilig, satt und fromm.

Du ewges Wollust-Meer, wann wirst
du mich recht tränken,
Und ganz und gar in dich und dei-
nen Blitz einschlukken?
Wann fällt das Fünklein, meine
Seele,
Ins Feuer deiner Gottheit ein?
Wann soll's sambt ihrer Leibes-Höle
Mit dir ein einge Flamme seyn?

Soul, distressed in sadness,
Doth rejoice with gladness,
Merged by Thee in heav'nly flood,
She's made holy, sated, good!

Ocean, Eternal lust, when will my
thirst be sated,
And thoroughly to Thee, O light-
ning, collated?
When falls my soul, that spark of
heaven,
In Thy eternal sacred flame?
When will she with her bod'ly cabin
And Thou, be fire, one, the same?

There is no reason for dwelling any longer on Angelus Silesius. Let us inspect two of his contemporaries who come quite close to a similar position. Among the forerunners of Pietism *Heinrich Müller* (1631-75) is entitled to a distinguished rank. Müller's poems, to an even greater degree than those of Angelus Silesius, are determined by the Song of Solomon. Here is no repentance of sin, no *Aus tiefster Not*, only a 'come, ye coarse audacious sinners', addressing itself to the unconverted. Certainly we hear even him speak in a smooth and sorrowful mood, but the reason for the sorrow is that the beloved bridegroom is nowhere to be found. The affliction of the Christian life is confined to this point. Characteristic in this respect are two songs, written quite complementarily, one of which mournfully complains that the soul's friend has stolen away and no more offers his sweetness for the soul's enjoyment, while the other rejoicingly proclaims his loving return:

| | |
|---|---|
| Er gab sich zu geniessen | He cometh and he blisses |
| Mit tausend Liebes Küssen, | With thousand loving kisses, |
| Den meine Seele liebt, | The lover of my soul, |
| Der mich vorhin betrübt. | Who just my pleasure stole. |

To Müller, as also, for example, to many of the Medieval mystics, the rhythm of the Christian life is determined by the fluctuating of the experience of loving sweetness, which now appears, now disappears. Communion with Christ is absorbed into, and identified with, the intensity of religious feeling.

The encounter with Christ is merely an occasion for the believer's immersing himself in the depths of his own emotions:

| | |
|---|---|
| Wann mich deine Liebes-Flammen, | When Thy love like blazing fire, |
| Süsser Jesu, zünden an, | Sweet Lord Jesus, kindles me, |
| Wann du Leib und Seel zusammen | Lifts my soul and body higher |
| Führest auff den Wollust-plan, | To eternal lust with Thee, |
| So bricht alles, was in mir, | Then flows all which in me is, |
| Wie ein voller Strom herfür. | Forth like mighty streams of bliss. |

A more significant hymn writer, however, is *Ahasverus Fritsch* (1629-1701). As to modes and expressions Fritsch seems more dependent upon the ecclesiastical tradition than is, for instance, Müller. Thus he forces us to face the problem of what significance to attribute to traditional Lutheran phrases in the writings (or in the speech) of a man who otherwise seems to favor concepts clearly incompatible with the original meaning of these phrases. Are the expressions mere arabesques and unaccentuated reminiscences, or do they indicate some underlying view with which they are in fact consistent? This question, of course, can only be answered with reference to each single case as it arises. A stanza like this sounds truly evangelical.

| | |
|---|---|
| Weil du zu erst mich hast geliebt, | Because Thou lovedst me first will I |
| Wil ich dich lieben wieder. | Truly in love adore Thee. |
| Ich habe dich zwar sehr betrübt, | How often did I Thee defy! |
| Doch fall ich für dich nieder | Now fall I down before Thee |
| Und bitte dich | And pray to Thee |
| Herz-inniglich: | Most heartily: |
| Lass Gnade für Recht gehen, | Let grace, not justice, sentence, |
| Wie könt ich sonst bestehen? | And see my poor repentance. |

But unfortunately the same author, in a far less traditional style, also happens to express a directly contrary view:

| | |
|---|---|
| Meinen treuen Jesum liebet | All my love and feelings tender |
| Mein Hertz nunmehr ganzt allein | To my Jesus now apply, |
| Und sich ihm in Lieb ergiebet, | Me in love to Him surrender |
| Wil auch ewig treu ihm seyn; | Faithfully to stand Him nigh. |
| Es hat sich so hoch verbunden, | This, my heart, be thy endeavor: |
| Ihn zu lieben, ihn zo loben alle | Him to love and Him to laud now |
| Stunden. | and ever! |

| | |
|---|---|
| Jesum lieb ich, Jesum lob ich, | Loving Jesus, lauding Jesus, |
| Jesum lass ich nimmermehr. | Leaving Jesus never more. |
| Auff ihn leb ich, auff ihn sterb ich, | Living on Him, dying on Him, |
| Nach ihm mich verlanget sehr. | Longing for him to restore. |
| Mein Hertz hat sich hoch verbun- | This, my heart, be thy endeavor etc. |
| den etc. | |

| | |
|---|---|
| Drumb, O Jesu, meine Liebe, | Therefore, O beloved Jesus, |
| Lieb auch du hergegen mich, | In return love even me. |
| Treu und Liebe an mir übe | Show me faithful, sweet affection |
| Immer und beständiglich, | Ever and unceasingly, |
| Weil mein Hertz sich hoch verbun- | As my heart has this endeavor, |
| den etc. | Thee to love and thee to laud now |
| | and forever! |

35

Here it is quite evident, firstly, that the poet unhesitatingly proclaims Jesus to be the only object of his sincere love, secondly, that he asks for the love of the Savior as a rather suitable as well as expected reward. The German words *Drumb, hergegen* and *weil* in the last stanza speak out quite unambiguously. The heading placed over the poem is this: *Jesus-Liebe und Gegen-Liebe* (Jesus-love and love-in-return). And the notion *Jesus-Liebe* does not at all mean the love Jesus has for man, but our love for him. So the point of this hymn can be no other than this: 'Let my unconditional love for Thee, O Jesus, be rewarded by Thy correspondingly true and faithful love for me.' But then does a writer like Fritsch not know that 'we love, because He loved us first'? Of course he does, in a certain sense. But the love he is speaking of here is not exactly that of a salutary power that has manifested itself once for all. It is the event that occurs when the hidden bridegroom decides to leave his hiding place to see and embrace his bride who has been searching for him in the garden and weeping and sobbing for not finding him. It is this moment of ecstatic happiness that the bride invokes:

O Jesu! mein Bräutgam, wie ist mir so wohl,
Dein Liebe, die macht mich ganz truncken und voll.
O selige Stunden!
Ich habe gefunden.
Was ewig erfreuen und sättigen soll.


Du hast mich, O Jesu! recht reichlich erquickt
Und an die Trost-Brüste der Liebe gedrückt.
Mich reichlich beschencket,
Mit wollust geträncket,
Ja gäntzlich in himmlische Freude verzückt.


O Jesus, my bridegroom, what pleasures are mine!
Thy love makes me drunk, I am Thine, I am Thine.
What bliss I acquire,
I found my desire,
Eternal and sweet satisfaction is mine!

Thou, Jesus, abundant refreshment hast brought,
And here at Thy breast I have found what I sought,
In lust I am merging,
In joy'ness resurging,
In heavenly raptures surpassing all thought.

Consideration of these three poets has given us a fairly distinctive impression of an experience of Christ which radically parts from the one we have studied in the hymns of Martin Luther. Whereas Luther is an heir, above all, to the basic motifs in the hymnody of the Ancient church, dawning Pietism finds its favorite motifs in Bernardian bride-mysticism and, through it, in the Song of Solomon. The road from Medieval mysticism to Pietism with its various byways is too complicated to be adequately uncovered in this essay. That such a road exists, and that it has been much travelled upon, should, however, be clearly demonstrated in the work of our three poets.

## 3.

The task we are undertaking next is that of throwing some light upon the transition from Luther to Fritsch in Lutheran hymnody by examining the idea of communion with Christ in the work of the two most outstanding hymn writers of the seventeenth century, *Johann Heermann* and *Paulus Gerhardt*. How are these two men placed in relation to the two poles we have described?

It is obvious enough that during most of the seventeenth century two different epochs, we might say, existed side by side without ever being organically united. Which of the *Kirchenlieder* of the time is the first to signal a transition from Reformation to Pietism? Some have pointed at 'Jesus, priceless treasure' (1650), others at 'How brightly beams the morning star' (1599). In fact, it seems to me, we might go back past Johann Franck and Philipp Nicolai all the way to Luther's close friend and collaborator, the musician *Johann Walter*, a clever composer, a very fine poet, but definitely not a theologian. The most sublime of his hymns is no doubt his *Herzlich thut mich Verlangen,* of which a few selected stanzas are presented in the new American Lutheran hymnal as 'Thy word, O God, declareth ...'. In this hymn the celestial wedding celebration of the Lamb is depicted in strong colors, but an underlying realistic eschatological tension prevents the pictures from becoming metaphorical vehicles for emotional extravagances; the wedding can scarcely be a metaphor of some satisfaction here and now of our, supposedly spiritual, desires. The same excellent compliment, however, cannot be given to another of his poems, which, in order to safeguard himself, he has felt the need of explaining in a preceding remark: 'This song profane may seem to you, but it is spiritual all through.'

| | |
|---|---|
| Holdselig meines hertzen trost, | O, charming comfort of my heart, |
| Mein Blümlein von der liebe, | My love, my blooming flower, |
| Dein lieb mich hat aus not erlost, | Thy love from sorrow took me 'part, |
| Darumb will ich mich uben. | Therefore shall all my power |
| Das ich Ie Lenger Ie Lieber dich | Swell in Thy love incessantly, |
| Von hertzen möcht gewinnen, | My heart Thy friendship praising, |
| Bey dir mich frewen ewiglich, | Rejoice in Thee eternally, |
| In deiner liebe brinnen. | In Thy affection blazing. |

| | |
|---|---|
| Liebeuglein und fein gilbig har | Sweet eyes and lovely yellow hair, |
| Hastu, die mir gefallen, | Thou hast, and how they please me! |
| Dein Mund ist rot mit Purpur zwar, | Thy lips are red with purple air, |
| Der liebet mir für allen, | No love like Thine can seize me. |
| Ich dencke an dich Tag und Nacht, | Of Thee I'm dreaming day and night, |
| Von deiner lieb ich singe, | Thy love I praise in singing, |
| Mein seel und geist dein frölich lacht, | My soul and ghost are filled with |
| Für freuden offt ich springe. | light, |
| | Myself from joy is springing. |

| | |
|---|---|
| Mein höchster schatz, ich bitte dich, | My treasure, I do pray to Thee, |
| Du wölst dich mein erbarmen. | Thou wouldst be mercy showing; |
| Gib mir dein kuss und hertze mich, | Give me Thy kiss and caress me, |
| Lass mich bey dir erwarmen. | Thy warmth unto me flowing. |
| Und wöllest, wie ich hoff zu dir, | And do, as I desire now, |
| In deinen schutz mich fassen, | Take me unto protection; |
| Mit hülffe, lieb und gunst gegn mir, | Me help and love and favor show, |
| Mich nimmermehr verlassen. | And never dereliction. |

The road from here to Angelus Silesius is still fairly long; but, clearly, the first steps are already taken. Or, we should rather say, it turns out that even in the circle of his closest friends and co-operators, Luther's vision had not totally swept out Medieval traces. The field has been weeded, but when we look back at it, we find here and there some little stalk indicating that the roots are still there, and that we might have to do the whole weeding over again in the not too distant future. Even Johann Walter expresses an enjoyment of the sweetness of Christ which is without any connection whatsoever with his belief in the real love of Christ, in the justifying grace. Walter seems to depict a source of joy *besides* the faith in forgiveness of sins.

When we proceed to examine the hymns of *Johann Heermann* (1585-1647), we find a distinctly unbridged dualism. In some connections communion with Christ is apparently integrated into a *fruitio*-pattern. In other connections it is clearly the Lutheran experience of forgiveness which is the alpha and the omega of his song. And, as a whole, it seems to me that this experience is the deepest personal concern of the poet. It may be of some significance that the one poem where, more than anywhere else in his output, mystical expressions prevail, was written at the order of, and according to a sketch presented by another man. The assessor von Koltwitz probably paid him not too bad a fee for his able pen:

Durch deine Krafft treff ich das
                Ziel,
Dass ich, so viel ich sol und wil,
Dich allzeit lieben könne.
Nichts auff der ganzen weiten Welt,
Pracht, Wollust, Ehre, Frewd vnd
                Geld,
Wann ich es recht besinne,
Kann mich
Ohn dich
Gnugsam laben.
Ich muss haben
Reine Liebe;
Die Tröst, wann ich mich betrübe.

Thy pow'r has brought me to my
                aim,
Which is my joy and is Thy claim:
I do sincerely love Thee.
Now nothing on this earthly globe,
Joy or desire, glorious robe,
Count. But the things above me.
Give Thee
To me,
Thou my treasure
And my pleasure,
See I'm needing
The pure love from Thee proceed-
                ing.

Especially in connection with Holy Communion, though, it seems that the idea of a static fruition of the celestial love has not been entirely foreign even to Heermann's own heart.

Kom, meine Frewde, kom,
    du schönste Krone!
Jesus, kom und in mir wohne!
In mir will ich dich mit Gebet offt
    grüssen,
Ja, mit Lieb und Glauben küssen.
Kyrieleison.
Bringe mit, was alle Welt erfrewt,
Deiner Liebe süsse Lieblichkeit,
Deine Sanfftmut vnd Geduld,
Die Frucht deiner Gnad und Huld.
Kyrieleison.

Come now, my joy, my crown, I do
    abide Thee,
Jesus, come and dwell inside me!
Here, in my heart, my prayers greet
    Thy blisses,
Hugging Thee with love and kisses.
Kyrie eleison.
Bring me the blessing from heav'n
    above,
The sweet communion of priceless
    love,
Thy affectionate smile,
Blossom of Thy mercy mild.
Kyrie eleison.

Or, somewhat more carefully expressed:

O sey und bleibe Mein! O sey und
    bleib in mir,
Unnd lass mich ewiglich auch seyn
    inn unnd bei dir.

O, stay forever mine, O, stay fore'er
    in me;
And let eternally myself remain in
    Thee.

Or:

Kom in mein Hertz, las mich mit dir
Vereinigt bleiben für und für.

Come in my heart, let me with Thee,
United be eternally.

Heermann, showing a certain preference of his own, seeks his models and expressions from men like Augustin, Bernard and Tauler. In a versification of one of *Johann Arndt*'s prayers, he can even say:

Wie ein Breutgam seiner Braut,
Wann er mit Liebe sie anschawt,
Sich frewet inniglich,
Also hastu auch in dir,
O Gott, Lust und Frewd an mir.
Ey so gib, dass ich auch mich
Frew, so offt ich denck an dich.

Like a bridegroom does abide
So joyfully his lovely bride,
Enraptured her to see;
Rejoicest Thou in me,
O God, abundantly;
Grant that even at Thy sight
I rejoice in full delight.

And the accomplishment and significance of Jesus may be expressed in seemingly mystical-pantheistic terms:

Liebster Schatz, Immanuel,
Du beschützer meiner Seel.
Gott mit vns in aller Not,
Neben vns und in vns Gott ...

Treasure dear, Immanuel,
Thou that in my soul dost dwell;
God with us in all our need,
'Round us and in us, indeed.

But certainly the same Johann Heermann has another and entirely different profile. With overwhelming power and clarity he expresses the basic theme we have studied in Luther's *Geistliche Lieder.* In a Christmas carol he points very impressively to the contrast between the fate Christ throws himself into in this world and the fate he has come to make us participants of. Poor in a manger — rich in heaven; born in a dark stall — led to the glorious hall of heaven; Thou comest into this world to me — I in the heavenly world to Thee; fettered in ropes — delivering me from the chains of Satan. And on this background emerges the praise:

Du hast kein Wieglein in der Welt:
O kom, mein Herz ist dir bestellt,
Leg dich hinein mit deiner Gnad,
Dass mir kein Todt noch Teuffel
                            schad.

No cradle in this world Thou hast.
O, come, my heart shall be Thy rest.
Stay with Thy grace, and I am free
From devil, death and slavery ...

And what profound evangelical experience does not speak through the stanzas of 'Ah, holy Jesus' (the heading a rather poor rendering of *Herzliebster Jesus*); the shepherd who suffers death for his sheep, the innocent Lord who dies for his guilty slaves. A peculiar but, according to modern concepts, not too tasteful testimony to the conformity of his faith in Christ, is his poem 'The purple red bloodworm' *(Blut-würmelein),* from Psalm 22, v. 7.' Jesus speaks to the faithful: In my sufferings I was scorned like a bloodworm, and in my pains I certainly had to writhe like one. But the blood has become my royal scarlet. And thus I can be a comforter for thee, even if thou art a sinful worm which Satan is driving down onto his dungheap. And even if the worm (in German *Wurm* means also

41

snake') gnaws thy heart, remember it has been killed by exactly this same blood. And when at last thou art going to writhe like a worm in death, so 'take me, humble worm, to thee, thy heart's my shrine eternally'; remember as thy comfort that even I writhed like a worm while swallowing thy death. When, at last, thy body definitely is going to become food for worms, I will take thee up again and dress thee in my royal scarlet. This, as can be seen, is theologically rather profound, but aesthetically at least somewhat questionable.

We feel more at home in the expressions of one of his Easter hymns, where, after having hailed the resurrection of Christ, he goes on:

| | |
|---|---|
| Jetzt ist der Tag, da micht die Welt | Today the world with anger gross |
| Mit schmach am Creutz gefangen helt. | Does keep me pris'ner on the cross. |
| Drauff folgt der Sabbath in dem Grab, | Then comes the Sabbath in the grave, |
| Darinn ich Ruh und Frieden hab. | A peaceful rest in sacred nave. |
| | |
| Er nehrt, er schützt, Er tröstet mich, | He does protect, comfort, relieve; |
| Sterb ich, so nimbt Er mich zu sich. | In darkest death he'll me receive. |
| Wo er jetzt lebt, da mus ich hin, | To where he lives, I shall be led, |
| Weil ich ein Glied seins Leibes bin. | For I am member, he is head. |

Or take this Lenten stanza:

| | |
|---|---|
| Auf dich setz ich mein Vertrawen, | All my faith I Thee surrender, |
| Du bist meine Zuversicht; | All my comfort Thou shalt be; |
| Dein Todt hat den todt zerhawen, | And Thy death cut death asunder, |
| Dass er mich kan tödten nicht. | So it is no death to me. |
| Dass ich an dir habe theil, | Thou art now my precious share, |
| Bringet mir Trost, Schutz vnd Heyl. | Strength and consolation fair. |
| Deine Gnade wird mir geben, | And Thy grace is my protection, |
| Auferstehung, Liecht vnd Leben. | Light and life and resurrection. |

Johann Heermann, as these quotations indicate, is conspicuously determined by two different traditions: Medieval-Pietistic mysticism and the Reformatory discovery which cannot be labelled as any particular 'ism' at all. Quite contrary to Ahasverus Fritsch, for example, whom we have also seen characterized by the same ambiguity, Heermann is predominantly at his ease when moving in the tracks of the Reformation. As soon as he expresses himself in the modern fashion of his century, his poems become more general and impersonal in their phrasing. He does not possess the mystical fervor that flows over in the poems of Angelus Silesius or Heinrich Müller. But his voice gets firm and powerful as soon as he starts to describe Christ as Savior from sin, death and the realm of Satan. In its way the somewhat strange and peculiar poem on the 'purple red blood worm' shows in a rather striking manner where the poet himself stands and what his own heart is filled with.

Where, then, do we find *Paulus Gerhardt* (1607-76), who is generally recognized as the most outstanding hymn writer of the Lutheran church? In Gerhardt the two different complexes of themes seem to some extent integrated with each other. But even in his work the Reformatory emphasis is clearly the prevalent one. The love of Christ toward us — and here again his sufferings are  the main topic — is always underlined as prior and superior to our love for him. And the eschatological tension is never really abandoned: Christian joy and happiness do not become some static possession, Christian man is conceived through and through as happy *and* afflicted, loving God *and* not loving. But at the same time it is obvious that in Gerhardt's hymns the believer, to an extent quite unfamiliar to Luther, is attending to and fighting his own tempers and shifting humors. Gerhardt is a child of his time, which shows itself in the fact that he can sometimes forget the basic evangelical concerns for quite a while when dealing with the events of his personal inward life. You are always sure he is going to remember them again, but to some extent we may accuse him of being a precursor of other poets and devotional writers who, by and by, manage to forget them so long that only vague recollections remain somewhere at the back of their minds, and for some of them not even there.

Let us look, for example, at his Christmas carol, *Ich steh an deiner Krippen hier,* and let us, in doing this, bear in mind Luther's 'From heav'n above to earth I come'. Take just two stanzas:

Ich sehe dich mit freuden an
Vnd kan mich nicht satt sehen,
Vnd weil ich nun nicht weiter kan,
So thu ich was geschehen.
O dass mein sinn ein abgrund wär
Vnd meine seel ein weites meer,
Dass ich dich möchte fassen!

With pleasure I'm regarding Thee,
My view will ne'er be sated.
Thy beauty overpowers me,
Adored, long awaited!
O might my spirit and my soul
An ocean be, and this their goal:
That I might comprehend Thee.

Vergönne mir, O Jesulein,
Dass ich dein mündlein küsse,
Das mündlein, das den süssen wein,
Auch milch und honig-flüsse
Weit übertrifft in seiner krafft:
Es ist voll labsal, stärck und safft,
Der march vnd bein erquicket.

Grant unto me, O Jesus mine,
To kiss thy lips so bonny,
Thy lips which more than sweetest
wine
And milk and flowing honey
Do strengthen me where'er I step
With joy and comfort, might and
sap,
My inward all refreshing.

In one connection he speaks to the Savior: 'Oh pleasure sweet, O noble calm, O joy for souls most pious.' His most consistent performance as to mystical expressions is the hymn 'O, Jesus Christ, my fairest light' *(O, Jesus som har elsket meg)*, a versification of one of the prayers of *Johann Arndt.* The most interesting stanzas, from our present point of view, are significantly excluded in, for instance, our Norwegian hymnals.

O dass mein hertze offen stünd
Vnd fleissig möcht auffangen
Die tröpfflein bluts, die meine sünd
Im garten dir abdrangen!
Ach dass sich meiner augen brunn
Aufthät und mit viel stöhnen
Heisse thränen
Vergösse, wie die thun,
Die sich in liebe sehnen.

O, might my heart wide open be
And catch in dear possession
The drops that in Gethsemane
Thou shedst for my transgression!
O, were the sources of my eyes
Opened, and I lamented,
Tears presented
Like the distressful cries
Of men by love tormented!

O dass ich wie ein kleines kind
Mit weinen dir nachgienge
So lange, bis dein herzt entzündt
Mit armen mich umbfinge
Vnd deine seel in mein gemüth
In voller, süsser liebe
Sich erhübe
Vnd also deiner güt
Ich stets vereinigt bliebe.

O, might I like a little child
With tears pursue Thy traces,
Until at last Thy heart conciled
Thou heartily embracest
Me, and Thy soul into my mind
Flows filled with sweet affection.
Thy dilection
Eternally I find,
O, tender, sweet complexion.

| | |
|---|---|
| Ach zeuch, mein liebster, mich nach dir, | Then draw me, O my love, to Thee, |
| So lauf ich mit den füssen: | I hurry in Thy traces; |
| Ich lauf und wil dich mit begier | Because I will desirously |
| In meinem hertzen küssen. | Kiss Thee with soft embraces. |
| Ich wil aus deines mundes zier | The sweetness of Thy lips I will |
| Den süssen trost empfinden, | Adopt as my possession, |
| Der die sünden | My transgression |
| Und alles unglück hier, | And every worldly thrill |
| Kan leichtlich überwinden. | Thou forcest to recession. |

This hymn follows the text of Arndt quite closely. Therefore a very pointed difference in the second of the stanzas quoted becomes rather remarkable. The prayer of Arndt reads: 'that Thou grantest me to taste Thee, and unitest Thyself with me through the spiritual celestial wedding, that I might become one heart, one spirit and one body with Thee'. It seems obvious that Gerhardt, in spite of the many mystical expressions he has adopted, has felt a little annoyed by the 'spiritual, celestial wedding', and that for this reason he has intentionally amended and moderated the text. The picture of the weeping child running after the Lord and begging for his attention — no doubt more successful poetically than it is theologically — Gerhardt adopts from Arndt, but the identification of the celestial wedding of the Lamb with the climax of emotional mystical experience he has been unable to accept.

But in spite of some extravagances and misses as in these examples, Gerhardt's basis is clear: the self-sacrificing love of the Savior is the decisive point, the sinner's devoted adoration is just the thankful reflex, and it will find its perfect expression only in a life to come.

| | |
|---|---|
| Herr, mein hirt, brunn aller freuden, | Lord, my Shepherd, take me to Thee. |
| Du bist mein, Ich bin dein: | Thou art mine; I was Thine, |
| Niemand kann uns scheiden. | Even 'ere I knew Thee. |
| Ich bin dein, weil du dein leben | I am Thine, for Thou hast bought me; |
| Vnd dein blut Mir zu gut | |
| In den tod gegeben. | Lost I stood, but Thy blood |
| | Free salvation brought me. |

Du bist mein, weil ich dich fasse
Vnd dich nicht, O mein licht,
Aus dem hertzen lasse.
Lass mich, lass mich hingelangen,
Da du mich und ich dich
Lieblich werd umbfangen.

Thou art mine; I love and own
Thee,
Light of joy, ne'er shall I
From my heart dethrone Thee.
Savior, let me soon behold Thee
Face to face. May Thy grace
Evermore enfold me!

Süsses heyl, lass dich umbfangen;
Lass mich dir, Meine zier,
Vnverrückt anhangen.
Du bist meines lebens leben:
Nun kan ich Mich durch dich
Wol zu frieden geben.

Comfort sweet, let me embrace
Thee;
Grant me here, treasure dear
Ceaselessly to face Thee.
Thou art life, my life forever,
Thanks to Thee comforts me
Peace that fadeth never.

Ich will dich mit fleiss bewahren,
Ich wil dir Leben hier,
Dir wil ich abfahren.
Mit dir wil ich endlich schweben
Voller freud Ohne zeit
Dort im andern leben.

Never will on earth I leave Thee
Till in life's final strife,
Lord, Thou willst receive me.
Finally, with Thee be drifting
— beyond time, joy sublime —
Glory never shifting.

Ich aber, dein geringster knecht,
Ich sag es frey und mein es recht:
Ich liebe dich, doch nicht so viel,
Als ich dich gerne lieben wil.

But I, Thy humblest servant, Lord,
Will have to speak this honest
word:
The love Thou know'st I feel for
Thee
Is weaker than I'd have it be.

Der will is da, die krafft ist klein,
Doch wird dir nit zu wider seyn
Mein armes hertz, und was es kan
Wirst du in gnaden nehmen an.

The will is there, but not the might;
Though is acceptable in Thy sight
My heart and my performance poor
As does Thy mercy me assure.

A very clear example is the hymn 'A Lamb goes uncomplaining forth', where the inconceivable love of Christ is presented first, and then the sacrifice of thanksgiving:

Mein Lebetage wil ich dich
Aus meinem Sinn nicht lassen;
Dich wil ich stäts, gleich wie du
mich,
Mit Liebes-Armen fassen.

From morn till eve my theme
shall be
Thy mercy's wondrous measure;
To sacrifice myself for thee
Shall be my aim and pleasure.

Du solt seyn meines Hertzens Liecht,
Und wenn mein Herzt in stücken
                                bricht,
Solstu mein Hertze bleiben.
Ich wil mich dir, mein höchster
                                Ruhm,
Hiermit zu deinem Eygenthumb
Beständiglich verschreiben.

My stream of life shall ever be a
Current flowing ceaselessly,
Thy constant praise outpouring.
I'll treasure in my memory,
O Lord, all thou hast done for me,
Thy gracious love adoring.

Erweitre dich, mein Hertzens-



                                schrein,
Du solst ein Schatzhaus werden
Der Schätze, die viel grösser seyn
Als Himmel, Meer und Erden.
Weg mit dem Gold Arabia,
Weg Calmus, Myrrhen, Casia!
Ich hab ein bessers funden:
Mein grosser Schatz, Herr Jesu
                                Christ,
Ist dieses, was geflossen ist
Aus deines Leibes Wunden.

Now, do expand, shrine of my
                                heart
A treasury to cherish
For treasures which are far more
                                worth
Than all that here does perish.
Arabian gold, now get thee hence,
Away with myrrh and frankin-
                                cense —
They are but dust and ashes.
My treasure is, Lord Jesus now,
The healing flood that once did
                                flow
Out from Thy wounds most pre-
                                cious.

In all the different dispensations of life, the blood of Christ grants to the faithful a real assurance and confidence — this is the theme of the two concluding stanzas of the same hymn.

Joy in the midst of tribulation — that is the main theme in the hymnody of Gerhardt, to which he returns again and again. In many cases this joy is attributed to the certainty of God as Father and Governor more than to the belief in the atonement of Christ. Hymns like 'Commit whatever grieves thee' *(Befiehl Du deine Wege)* or 'Now be content and rest in comfort' *(Gib dir zufrieden und sei stille)* do not mention the name of Jesus at all. On the other hand, hymns like 'If God himself be for me' *(Ist Gott für mich so trete)* or 'Now arise to God, thy God' *(Schwing dich auf zu deinem Gott)* fully prove the basic importance of faith in Christ for Gerhardt's victory over tribulation. The central issue of his affliction is not quite constant: sometimes it is clearly the repentance of sins which is dominant, sometimes accidents or misfortunes of different kinds

47

that threaten to separate the Christian from God. Even in the latter aspect Gerhardt moves definitely away from Angelus Silesius in taking this life absolutely seriously. This 'world' and the many relations in which the believer finds himself placed, is not some kind of an illusion he has got to do away with in order to embrace the pleasures of celestial love. Resignation and sacrifice always hurt, adversities foster affliction because even *this* world is a God's world and its blessing God's blessing, which it is completely impossible for a Christian to regard with indifferent elevation. Christian existence is a joyful and painful education. In our daily life the death as well as the resurrection of Christ are present and affecting even *our* death (from sin) and *our* resurrection (to righteousness).

Let me — in this connection — just bring your attention to the following stanza from Gerhardt's *Auf, auf, mein Herz mit Freuden.*

| | |
|---|---|
| Ich hang und bleib auch hangen | To Christ attached forever, |
| An Christo als ein Glied. | His member now I am. |
| Wo mein Haupt durch ist gangen, | And where my head did travel, |
| Da nimt er mich auch mit. | He bringeth me with Him. |
| Er reisset durch den Tod, | Behold Him break through death, |
| Durch Welt, durch Sünd, durch Noth. | Through world, through sin, through wrath, |
| Er reisset durch die Höll, | Through hell victoriously! |
| Ich bin stäts sein Gesell. | Oh, blessed company! |

## 4.

Our round trip is finished. We have seen how some of the most influential hymn writers of the seventeenth century predominantly carry on the theme of Martin Luther, at the same time as they signal the transformation which was to be so overwhelming during the last decades of the century — a transformation in almost every area of church life, but probably most conspicuous precisely in the hymns and devotional literature. Obviously, Johann Arndt was one of the main channels for the influx of non-Lutheran mysticism into the Lutheran

48

church. But the components of causality in this setting are too many and too complicated to deal with in this essay.

The history of Lutheran hymnody from Luther up to 1700 reflects a definite theological turning from *Conformitas Christi* to *Fruitio Christi*. In Luther communion with Christ means that Christ undertakes to share our sin and condemnation and, thus doing, shares with us His righteousness and glory. In Scheffler, Müller and Fritsch the consciousness of sin is overcome in an entirely different way; the soul abandons its worldly pleasures and turns to its heavenly bridegroom to rejoice in the experience of mystical reunion. Heermann and Gerhardt — and many others — are basically on the side of Luther, but are also, and to a not unimportant extent, marked by the new era. The joy they proclaim is clearly derived from the forgiveness of sins. Only rarely does it seem to draw somewhat apart from the experience of forgiveness, and thus from faith, and become an independent possession of the pious heart. Heermann and Gerhardt seem to accept the expressions of their time without serious reflection upon their real contents. This is the way spiritual changes as a rule take place in history: they are brought about slowly and unconsciously by people who do not as yet realise what is happening, until one day some people become aware of what is already half completed and pledge themselves in a conscious commitment to it.

This is by no means to assert that the hymnody of the eighteenth century is *exclusively* dominated by a Christianity of 'fruition'. Even in the pietistic hymns we find much of the same dualism as in the hymnody of Orthodoxy. The very able Danish hymn writer Brorson, (e. g., 'Behold a host, like mountains bright') who, fortunately, is much more confused in his theology than is Angelus Silesius, once in a while proclaims the Gospel with the most brilliant clarity, then once in a while rejects it without nourishing the slightest suspicion of what he is doing.

The hymnody *reflects* the theology and preaching of the church. But it seems equally true to say that it *affects* them. The hymns are perhaps the most effective link connecting the theology of the church with the daily life of its members. No

4. Lønning.

doubt our churches ought to give a much deeper attention to this fact than has up to now usually been the case. I do not know of a single Lutheran hymnal which cannot genuinely be accused of containing a host of blatant 'heresies'.

I am touching here on a question that is far more serious for discussion on *pura doctrina* than are many of the quite heated quarrels which once in a while arise over that topic.

# III

## The Limits of Reason in the Thought of Blaise Pascal

Where should the uninitiated reader start his study of Pascal? Is there some peak from which a fairly consistent view of the vast field of his intellectual occupations can be enjoyed: physics, geometry, practical inventions, epistemology, psychology, theology, edifying writings? As far as I can see, there exists just one such peak: let the student start to read the *Conversation with M. de Sacy*. This extremely interesting and entertaining conversation between Blaise Pascal and one of the leading Jansenist priests must have taken place in the beginning of the year 1655. Although not too sophisticated in its abbreviated logical performances this conversation presents us with the entire philosophy of Pascal in a nutshell. Of course you cannot settle matters of dispute in contemporary study of Pascal by referring just to this short conversation, but certainly there are suggestions to be found here which are of paramount importance for our understanding.

In this conversation Pascal presents *Epictetus* and *Montaigne* as his favorite authors. They are, as he says, the most outstanding representatives of the only two possible ways of consistent human thinking: Epictetus, the thinker who believes in reason and in man as a reasonable creature; Montaigne, the thinker who does not believe. On the one hand, man realizing himself as part of an all-embracing structure of truth. On the other, man finding himself left alone with his own capriciousness, guided, not by reason, but only by the abhorrence of inconvenience.

In this conversation Pascal reduces the history of philosophy, indeed even the possibilities of philosophy, to these alternatives: affirming reason or denying reason. Which of the two does he acclaim as his own? As it happens, neither. His point is to affirm that both thinkers are right and therefore, of course, both wrong. What Pascal himself is looking for is a possibility of uniting both viewpoints, not by way of a mutual modification, but by a dialectical combination through which they assert each other's truth and destroy each other's claim of possessing the whole truth.

I shall refrain from commenting upon these presuppositions. Let us be content with remarking that Pascal is obviously correct at least in observing that most thinkers seem to be basically concerned with either an extension or a reduction of the competency generally attributed to rational understanding by their milieu. Some construct systems of assurances, others tear them down — even if no thinker has ever been involved in a one hundred per cent constructive or one hundred per cent destructive activity, the two types — the philosophical constructor and the philosophical destroyer — are easily recognizable throughout the entire history of thought. Though the distinction as such seems to me to be perhaps of fundamental interest more in a psychological or a sociological setting than in an epistemological one, in the work of Pascal it acquires an epistemological significance through the dialectical opposition into which it is thrown.

Pascal decides to make a conscious attempt at breaking what seem to him to be two coherent ranks of philosophical tradition, by putting them together and in opposition at the same time. In whichever context Pascal approaches the problems of human cognition we shall have to keep this basic in-between position in mind.

1.

Even if it involves certain dangers to frame the thoughts of a philosopher in terms of notions which are not his and to which others have given meanings certainly unfamiliar to him, it may sometimes be necessary for compendiousness and for brevity. This is my only excuse for presenting Pascal's tracing of the limits of reasons in the following sentence, which will be developed during the rest of this lecture: *Pascal's conception of the limitation of reason proceeds from a fourfold consideration, with a logical, an ontological, a psychological, and a theological application.* I freely admit that the limits between these four contexts in the work of Pascal are not sharp and clearcut; my choice of number as well as my choice of names may therefore be judged as somewhat arbitrary. However, for the reason already given I regard my choice as justifiable, even if I should be found to be incapable of justifying it.

In order to get an impression of Pascal's conception of logic, we shall turn to his unfinished sketch 'On the Geometrical Spirit'. Here Pascal gives an exposition of what in his opinion would have been the perfect scheme of scientific reasoning. Indeed there exists no science which can fulfill the two ideal claims; the one that comes closest is geometry. The claims are for definitions of all notions and proofs of all propositions. Why cannot all notions be defined or all propositions proved? Simply because a definition of a notion presupposes other notions to define with; these notions again, of course, must be defined before they can be used for defining others. We have to go backward and seek definitions of the concepts we use in our definitions, and definitions behind these definitions, and so on. We are engaged in a *regressus in infinitum*; there exists no absolute starting point by means of which reason is able to assert itself. And as to the proving of propositions, the situation is exactly the same: a proof presupposes propositions already established by other proofs, and so on *ad infinitum*.

In the *Pensées* the same predicament is pointed out as the special point made by people called 'Pyrrhonists', a term originating from the Greek skeptic Pyrrho and frequently used in the seventeenth century to refer to those who doubted the appropriateness of human thought. The Pyrrhonists stick to reason, Pascal states, and by means of reason they seem to destroy every piece of real assurance. But — as you might have suspected — Pascal does not leave his Pyrrhonists victorious.

Certainly they have clearly understood how reason operates, but there is one thing they have overlooked. What is that? It is 'nature'. Nature — that is the really unconquerable point of the dogmatists. Who are they? The Neo-Stoics, disciples of Epictetus. There exist in the human mind some basic *a priori* concepts. Time — space — number — movement — matters which can be neither proved nor defined by reason are presuppositions which human reason can never abstract from. Reason cannot conquer these natural concepts, but neither can it flee from them without abolishing itself. What reason finds itself presupposing and unable to abolish without abolishing every possibility of its own operation — which would ultimately have been self-contradictory because reason in abolishing its own possibility of operation is obviously still operating — it has got to accept *de facto*. The flaw of the dogmatists is to exaggerate this natural cognition and to make of it an insight into the very essence of things. This is a piece of mere superstition, which reason easily refutes. Nature and reason, dogmatists and Pyrrhonists, thus confirm and defeat one another at the same time.

Isn't this really rather cheap? To let the champions kill each other violently and then to step out on the field and proclaim oneself victor? In order to see this in a proper light it might be a good idea to compare the victory won by Pascal with that won by his senior contemporary *Descartes*. Like Pascal Descartes follows the destructive regress of reason and asks how, after all, real assurance could be established. Descartes intends to follow the dissolutive movement of reason *ad infinitum*: *De omnibus dubitandum est*. But in doubting everything he becomes aware that doubt itself involves a basic assurance: No doubt without a doubting thought, no thought without a thinking I, no thinking I without participation in a universal thought, no universal thought unless it gives a meaning even to the singular phenomena — so, after all, I trust my senses because I trust that the universal divine being would not deceive me.

There are indications that Pascal really considered the possibility of joining the Cartesian track. But he did not. 'What shall I do,' he asks in *Pensées*, 'shall I doubt everything?' No. And why not? Because such a doubt has never existed and can never come to exist. Even radical doubt in everything presupposes something toward which it has not turned its critical eye. In order to doubt you must have something you don't doubt, just as a body cannot move except in relation to something which is not included in its own movement. To be consistent Cartesian doubt must become a mere fiction. The rabbit Descartes pulls out of his top hat was certainly hidden in the hat beforehand.

Now it is not easy to see which interpretation of the Cartesian *Cogito* is the appropriate one. I think we should even consider the possibility that Descartes intended to say the very same thing as Pascal, namely, Given the intention to have doubt in everything, where would this take me? Whether you say such radical doubt is an impossibility or you analyze it and find it has overcome itself, may be of little consequence. The basic difference between the two thinkers is not to be found here. Even if the turning point from doubt to assurance might be the same in either of them, the assurance they turn to is not the same. Descartes has found a starting point for an all-comprehensive series of deductions. But Pascal has shown that reason, in order to operate, has to accept its ultimate evidence outside itself. Intuitive knowledge and reflective knowledge presuppose each other, but there is a basic difference in the manner in which they are achieved. This difference never occurred to Descartes. His thought is like a boomerang, it is flung out in the fog of skepticism and returns to assurance all by itself. The thought of Pascal is like a ball hitting a wall and bouncing back. This wall is the wall of factual experience.

To Pascal the logical performance does not rest in itself in the way it seems to for Descartes. Its operation is limited, and the first limitation we have noted is the dependence upon certain basic notions prior to and constitutive of any logical achievement. Already, from the very structure of reasoning, it is shown that reason must depend upon something outside itself. For otherwise the logical process would just have been lost in its own infinity.

But even if human understanding can thus escape the infinity of logical display, there is another infinity which is far more difficult to handle, the infinity of the physical universe. Pascal, like the other outstanding physicists of his century, is consistently an infinitist. The infinitism of the seventeenth century is inspired by those new and powerful instruments, the telescope and the microscope. Basically, however, it does not rest upon factual evidence, but upon the *a priori* assumption that there exists no such thing as a spatial maximum or minimum — any space can be increased or diminished. To Descartes and his school this is a clear and consistent idea, fitting brilliantly into the basic logical structure which bestows validity even upon our factual observations, and obviously in itself compatible with these observations. The perfect expression of this concept of infinity is given by *Spinoza*: in his thought the very idea of infinity is the one that guarantees the validity of our finite ideas; it becomes, in other words, the cornerstone of human assurance.

To Pascal infinity seems a far more complicated thing to get along with. To him infinity is not primarily an idea held in perfect possession by the human mind, it is the universe that man finds himself flung into. It is the thing man cannot comprehend, but which comprehends him — to express it in Pascal's own way. Not infinity itself, but man in the grasp of infinity, is the subject of Pascal's meditation — and that makes quite a difference. In this scheme man occurs midway between infinity and nothing. Compared with the wonders studied through the telescope he becomes a mote of dust; compared with the no less astonishing wonders revealed through the microscope he becomes himself a universe. 'For, in fact, what is man in nature? A Nothing in comparison with the Infinite, an All in comparison with the Nothing, a mean between nothing and everything. Since he is infinitely removed from comprehending the extremes, the end of things and their beginning are hopelessly hidden from him in an impenetrable secret; he is equally incapable of seeing the Nothing from which he was made, and the Infinite in which he is swallowed up.' (*Pensées*, Brunschvicg's classification No. 72.)

To Spinoza the idea of infinity guarantees the validity of his entire thought. To Pascal the meditation of man in infinity puts a question mark to all our cognitive accomplishments: how can we be sure we know a matter when the total pattern of which it is a part is completely hidden from us? Pascal here opposes the dogmatists' idea of infinity as a kind of bridge between the human mind and reality in its fullness — a conception which has been predominant within the Western Platonic tradition which was so powerfully revived in the Renaissance. The Pyrrhonists of the time were inclined either to reject the infinity of space or to take up an agnostic position. Determined as they were by late Medieval Nominalism they took note of only singular phenomena and considered every attempt at establishing general patterns as arbitrary.

Even in this respect the position of Pascal is an in-between one. As a geometrician he felt obliged to admit the infinity of space, but to him this infinity is a *terminus ad quem* that he is always approaching from the side of finitude; it is a borderline he can never get beyond. He knows it is there, but its essence and its possible 'meaning' remain hidden from him. Infinity cannot be changed through the addition or the subtraction of finite entities, and thus our categories simply do not apply.

Thus the concept of infinity forbids physics to transcend itself and turn into metaphysics. The knowledge of physical phenomena we can gain through experience is real enough, but the pretensions of this knowledge must be modest. Because reflection tells us that infinity is there, and that we are simply fenced in by infinity, it also tells us that the possible meaning of our existence cannot be revealed by intellectual operations. Thus it occurs that 'The eternal silence of these infinite spaces frightens me' (Br. 206). But it also involves a kind of a promise, because it proves that the existence of a phenomenon does not depend just on its comprehensibility. It makes, for example, any proof of the existence of God invalid, God being even more inconceivable than the infinite space which, after all, has the quality of spatial extension in common with us. But, at the same time, it offers a vigorous demonstration that 'We may well know the existence of a thing without knowing its nature ... We know then the existence and nature of the finite, because we also are finite and have extension. We know the existence of the infinite and are ignorant of its nature, because, like us, it has extension, but, unlike us, no limits. But we know neither the existence nor the nature of God, because he has neither extension nor limits.' (Br. 233.)

In facing the infinity of space, reason has discovered its second limitation. In the context of logical analysis reason found itself dependent upon an area outside its own reach: the axioms of intuitive cognition. These tools it receives as gifts from 'Nature' — tools which are absolutely necessary but which are in themselves no real cognitive accomplishments. It is up to reason itself to use the tools and fulfill their purpose. But, also, the discovery of infinite space involves a limit to the scope of reason and a radical reduction of its immediate pretensions. At the same time, however, there is a confirmation of the use and the necessity of reason within the limits traced. The dogmatists' exploitation of the concept of infinity and the Pyrrhonists' scorn both miss man's meeting with infinity: the awe of the *'silence éternel de ces éspaces infinis'*.

## 3.

The third setting where a definite limitation of the intellectual operation occurs, is the one I have named the 'psychological'. According to the classical tradition of Western thought, there exist two main faculties in man: the faculty of love and the faculty of understanding. Let us point out how these were conceived in their relationship to one another by the different schools of thought in the seventeenth century. By the Neo-Stoics they were regarded as, in principle, identical. *Bonum* and *verum*, the good and the true, cannot be separated from each other. Either you understand the all-comprehensive structure of nature *and* you love it, or you neither love nor understand. To the Thomist tradition, which was definitely losing its influence from year to year, it was a basic concern to distinguish and, to a certain extent at least, safeguard the primacy of intellectual operation. Reason is the capacity for connecting factual observations and for discovering their pattern. Even if a full comprehension of the essence of reality cannot be attained except by divinely inspired love, rational observation provides a distinctive approach to it: reason proceeds by means of analogy from stage to stage toward the top of the pyramid. To reason itself this top is indeed hidden above an impenetrable cloud, but by observing faithfully the lower part which is fully visible beneath that cloud, it is not at all impossible to trace the outline of the rest. Thus intellectual operation becomes a very important preparation for the inspiration of that love which confers perfect understanding.

A somewhat different outlook is advocated by the Augustinian movement, which exercised a tremendous influence in French seventeenth-century philosophy. '*Le siècle de S. Augustin*', this age has recently been called by a distinguished French scholar (Dagens). In this philosophical current a lot of theologically irreconcilable groups mingle: Jansenists, Jesuits, Malebranchians, to some extent even Cartesians, likewise many of the Montaigne-influenced skeptics of that age. According to this tradition, love exercises a more basic influence upon human life and opinions than does the intellect. Will and reason, says a philosopher of the age, are like a blind squire and his seeing servant. The squire needs the servant in order to reach his goals, but it is definitely the squire himself who sets the goal. According to *Montaigne*, reason is an attorney that man summons every time he needs someone to excuse and justify the choices of his will. To some Augustinians, such as Father Yves de Paris, the great hero of liberal Augustinian authors in France in our century (Bremond, Chesneau and others), who come quite close to Neo-Stoicism, this will is a natural desire for the ultimate good. To others, who are more influenced by Montaigne, it is a blind quest for the satisfaction of our different and constantly changing passions. The objects of our love are determined by the customs of the milieu we are reflecting, by our private habits, by our profound desire for convenience. To the Jansenist movement, to which Pascal was affiliated, the will is in a certain sense both things at the same time: a capacity of total surrender and commitment, created for uniting man with his Maker, and corrupted by treacherous commitment to this world with its fleshly lusts and its spiritual arrogance.

In all these profoundly incompatible Augustinian schools there is a common understanding of the bearing of unconscious factors upon human consciousness. We think the way we think because we are the way we are, and we are the way we are because we desire the things we desire.

In a characteristic manner this understanding reflects itself in the writings of Pascal. Take, for instance, this famous and frequently abused quotation from *Pensées*: 'The heart has its reasons, which reason does not know. We feel it in a thousand things. I say that the heart naturally loves the Universal Being, and also itself naturally, according as it gives itself to them; and it hardens itself against one or the other at its will. You have rejected the one and kept the other. Is it by reason that you love yourself?' This is the full quotation. 'Reasons of the heart', to Pascal, is no romantic expression asserting that there is no use in reason and that we should just go ahead and do what our passions require of us. This is the way it is usually misunderstood, as, for example, by the Duchess of Windsor who borrowed the sentence for the title of her autobiography. Pascal does not at all praise, laud and magnify the reasons of the heart. On the contrary, he is pointing at the rather disgraceful fact that thought, which in other connections he has said constitutes the very humanity of man, does not at all determine our attitude toward the realities basically determining our lives.

What is the 'heart'? We have no time for stating satisfactorily the very interesting history of this term. No doubt its basic orientation is to be found in the Old Testament writings, where it is not intended to signify just one particular psychological activity as distinct from others, but to point out the wholeness of human inward life. The most appropriate substitute for the Biblical expression 'my heart' is simply 'I'. The orientation of the term is predominantly affective, but a certain cognitive relevance is obvious enough. In Pascalian terminology the intuitive knowledge of principles as well as the commemorative knowledge of something once acquired by reason, may both be attributed to the heart. (Cf. also the English expression, 'to know by heart'.) In *Pensées* the knowledge of the heart is knowledge proceeding from or integrated into a man's self-consciousness, a knowledge which cannot be omitted without effecting a change in that entity which I experience as my 'I'.

What this means may, I expect, be clarified through a study of the most famous of all the *Pensées* fragments, the one representing the argument usually known as 'the wager of Pascal' (Br. 233). This fragment starts, 'Our soul is cast into a body, where it finds number, time, dimension. Thereupon it reasons, and calls this nature and (!) necessity, and can believe nothing else'. As you will have noticed, this is exactly the supposition we have notified as the 'logical' termination of reason: reason simply has to accept *de facto* some basic concepts which it cannot get beyond. After this follows a short development of the 'ontological' termination: infinity is a fact which reason cannot measure, but which it has got to accept anyhow. And the conclusions are derived: the existence of God cannot be proved, but some things which cannot be proved we have to accept as existing all the same.

After this preface Pascal starts an argument with an unbeliever. As reason cannot determine the existence of God, it must attempt to settle the dispute between religious belief and unbelief by solving another problem: the problem as to which of the alternatives would be most preferable to man if, in this matter as in all others, he were to 'consult his private ends'. Like the gambler at the gaming-table, man facing religion can give no rationally motivated prediction of the outcome. But he can consider two things: the probability of gain, and the proportion between the bet and the gain. The joint consideration of the proportion and the probability makes possible a mathematical calculation of the odds.

Here there exists no possibility of staying outside the wager:

'you are already embarked'. The bet for or against God offers a probability of one to one and a proportion of gain of one to infinity. Therefore the calculation should be easy enough: reason tells you definitely to bet *for* the existence of God.

This argument has been seriously criticized by many commentators. Characteristic is the judgment of *William James*: 'We feel that a faith . . . adopted willfully after such a mechanical calculation would lack the inner soul of faith's reality; and if we were ourselves in the place of the Deity, we should probably take particular pleasure in cutting off believers of this pattern from their infinite reward.' (*The Will to Believe*, 1899, p. 6.) But this criticism is founded on a fundamental misunderstanding of Pascal's argument. This becomes clear through an examination of the rest of the fragment. Pascal's interlocutor admits that the argument as such seems valid, but this does not help him to believe: 'I have my hands tied and my mouth closed; I am forced to wager, and am not free. I am not released, and am so made that I cannot believe.' What has Pascal to say to this? 'True, but at least learn that your inability to believe comes from your passions. Since reason brings you this and yet you cannot accept it, you must endeavor to convince yourself, not by increase of proofs of God, but by abatement of your passions.' The practical advice Pascal gives his partner, is to live as if he believed; thus he will certainly come to believe.

The purpose of the wager argument is not to serve as a convincing proof, but rather the opposite: to show that even the last, and logically valid onset of reason cannot make a man believe. What Pascal has intended to prove is that reason is incapable, not only of deciding whether God exists, but even of motivating a decision for belief or unbelief. It is not reason that prevents a man from believing, even if he himself claims it is. The decision must take place on another level; a man who in his daily life behaves as if God did not exist will never come to believe before having realized this predicament and having tried to behave as if God did exist. The function of reason is to unveil these circumstances and to trace the limits between the matters it is able to handle and those which are outside its

reach. Reason, and reason alone, can determine these limits. But if it refuses to do so it loses itself in hopeless involvement with the caprices and passions of the human heart.

The psychology of the Pascalian wager is definitely that of the Augustinian tradition. According to Augustine faith and love (which are consistently the same thing) must always precede rational understanding — *fides praecedat rationem* — but prior to this *fides* is another *ratio* which prescribes that faith must precede reason. This sounds rather facile, but the logical consistency is above doubt. Montaigne's discovery of human capriciousness has been important for the development of Pascal's adoption of this point, but even more so has the Cartesian concept of man as a synthesis of thought and automaton. According to this mechanistic psychology the human body is a machine, driven forward by its inherent passions. Spiritual reason lives in a kind of personal union with *la machine*. Thought and passion mutually affect each other through a unifying center in the human brain. The task of a human being is to accomplish the predominance of thought over passion, and the means of achieving this is meditation. But in the meantime it is useful to avoid any contamination of thought, and this can be done by means of a practical oppression of the passions. Even if Pascal does not approve of the theory of the unifying center, the concept of the 'machine' has been useful for him; in some of the *Pensées* we even find the term explicitly adopted.

More might have been said on this point. But probably this will do to suggest what I understand by the 'psychological' termination of reason in the work of Pascal.

4.

The last of the four limitations I suggested is the theological one. Let us straightaway ask how far Pascal shares the opinion, not infrequently advocated in Christendom, that, as a consequence of the Fall, reason has become corrupt.

As an answer, consider this passage from the *Pensées*: 'Nature corrupted — Man does not act by reason which constitutes his being.' In another connection and from an apparently quite contrary viewpoint, he can maintain that *cette belle raison corrompue a tout corrompu'* (cf. Br. 439 and Br. 294). We find a lot of seemingly contradictory assertions like this. What is the 'thought behind' these contradictions? In fact, it is not difficult to discover. To Pascal thought in itself is by no means corrupt. Thought is an instrument, very suited to its purpose. But, as already shown, thought is not an activity which takes place in isolation from the non-intellectual operations of the human mind; it is continually being summoned to defend and justify our desires. When it refuses to see its own limitation, when it performs the task our passions ask of it, namely, that of justifying and underwriting their own acts of unreason, then reason has become corrupt because it is enslaved by corrupt nature.

'Submission and the use of reason' is the heading of one of the bundles of notes Pascal left behind at his death, and which was to become part of the work known to posterity as *Pensées*. One of these notes reads as follows: 'Two extremes: to exclude reason, to admit reason only.' (Br. 253; note the dialectical combination.) And another: 'The last proceeding of reason is to recognize that there is an infinity of things which are beyond it. It is but feeble if it does not see so far as to know this. But if natural things are beyond it, what will be said of supernatural?' (Br. 267). This seems to be exactly the same assertion that Soeren Kierkegaard makes in *Concluding Unscientific Postscript* when he maintains: 'There exists something of which I clearly understand that I do not understand it.'

The depravity of reason in sinful man consists in its enslavement. It accepts its servitude in human pride and self-righteousness by refusing to see its own limits and the elusive powers which command its service. The able attorney sells his ability to a shameful cause; he is paid to convince human conscience that rational deliberations are the real source of human rebellion against God. But this rebellion was a *fait accompli* long before the attorney, before reason, was involved in the matter. The true task of reason, according to Pascal, is to undo this business, and to reveal the real forces behind human behavior. Reason should not justify human reactions, but discover them.

However, reason is only competent to reveal these reactions to a certain extent. Reason can prove that reason itself is not the cause of human unbelief and that man, in arguing as if it were, is mistaken. But to unveil this mistake is not precisely the same thing as to assent to the Christian concept of sin. Reason admits that reason is wrong in denying God, but it can by no means decide whether or not *man* is wrong in doing it, only that he is wrong in pleading reason for his choice. But admitting that Christianity is true, and that man really is opposing his Maker, then of course — as a result of the observations about the affiliation between reason and heart — it follows that even operations of reason adapt themselves to the general depravity of human existence; which gives yet another reason for the inability of reason to judge about the truth of Christianity.

In the *Thomist* tradition the possibility of a 'natural theology' is founded on the assumption that reason is a faculty clearly distinct from the passions and desires of the human heart. It can therefore function as a neutral inspector of human existence. Like other outstanding representatives of 'the century of St. Augustine', Pascal denies this assumption. Whereas 'nature' to the Thomists means the basic principle of things given in the creation, a principle fully recognizable to reason, 'nature' to the Augustinians does not stand for creational teleology but for factual complexity. According to a modern French interpreter, Pascal does not 'consider human nature in itself, but only in so far as it is tainted by sin' (Chesneau).

This does not at all mean that reason and religion are incompatible entities. Here, as elsewhere, reason, when keeping to its own preserve, is a reliable and necessary guide. But here, as elsewhere, it depends upon principles presented to it from outside its own reach. And because human personality in its fullness and complexity is concerned with religion as with no other realm of problems, the danger of an illegitimate enslavement is more acute here than anywhere else.

In the field of religion the Scylla and Charybdis of Pyrrhonism and dogmatism reveal themselves in the dispute between atheism and deism. According to atheism there is nothing whatsoever in nature that favors the belief in God. According to deism everything favors it. They both solve the religious issue without the least trouble or pain. But to a really alert observer both of them are right and both of them wrong. Here lies the real issue of Christianity. Man finds himself in a rather awkward predicament: he sees too much in favor to be able to deny, and too much in contradiction to be able to affirm. In the former fact lies his capacity for, in the latter his need of, a divine illumination, the gracious inspiration of love which makes man see by making him willing to see.

Like *Luther* and some of the Medieval mystics, Pascal loves the expression in the Latin translation of Isaiah xlv:15 *Vere, tu es deus absconditus* — 'Verily, Thou art a God that hidest Thyself'. To Pascal this reconditeness of God is due to what he calls the blindness of natural man; that is, to the incapacity of a man existentially opposed to God for knowing God — an assertion the background of which we have already demonstrated. But there is one thing still unmentioned which also contributes to the collapse of natural theology. In the document known as the *Memorial* of Pascal, a parchment which after his death was found sewn into his coat, and which reflects the tremendous overwhelmingness of a decisive religious experience, be expresses himself thus: 'God of Abraham, God of Isaac, God of Jacob, not of the philosophers and of the savants.' I don't think this means that philosophy students — or professors — are necessarily godless. What Pascal rejects are the philosophical notions of God, such as 'supreme being', 'supreme good', 'immovable mover of all', 'absolute idea' etc. The best comment given on the *Memorial* is this utterance from one of the *Pensées*: 'The God of Christians is not a God who is simply the author of mathematical truths, or of the order of the elements; that is the view of the heathens and the Epicureans. He is not merely a God who exercises His providence over the lives and fortunes of men, to bestow upon those who worship Him a long and happy life. That was the lot of the Jews. But the God of Abraham, the God of Isaac, the God of Jacob, the God of Christians, is a God of love and of comfort, a God who fills the soul and heart of those whom He possesses, a God who makes them conscious of their inward wretchedness and his infinite mercy . . .'

According to the French author *Sully Prudhomme*, there is a basic inconsistency in Pascal's conception of God. At the same time as Pascal was attracted by the philosophical idea of God, advocated by the Deists and the Cartesians of his age, he was emotionally bound to the primitive anthropomorphic conception favored by traditional religious practice, which definitely treats God as if he were some kind of a man, only on a somewhat large scale. It is some fifty years now since this judgment was passed. In the meantime the personalistic school of French philosophy ought to have made it clear that a personal concept of, and encounter with, the basic reality is by no means an inferior attitude to the conceptual objectification advocated by metaphysics. To Pascal God is not a thing, not even an abstract idea, which in this connection is just as much a 'thing' as is a stone or a tree or some other kind of fetish, which man can handle and make himself master of. God is Lord and Sovereign, therefore we cannot fence him in by means of concepts and definitions. But certainly our concepts can render us important assistance in the clarification of our own relationship to God, and in the discovery of a multitude of false pretensions which usually influence this relationship.

A brief summary in conclusion: We have seen that limitations of reason derive from four different sets of presuppositions: logical, ontological, psychological, theological. For the sake of space, the description has necessarily been subject to radical simplifications. However, I earnestly hope that this sketch leaves the reader with at least some slight impression of the tremendous intellectual effort behind Pascal's approach to the problem of human knowledge.

His dialectical effort to combine and overcome the logically consistent but empirically insufficient presuppositions of skepticism and dogmatism has rendered a very useful stimulus and instigation to the thought of our own century. With good reason the English author *D. M. Eastwood* twenty-seven years ago entitled her study of the influence of Pascal on French literature during the preceding seventy-five years, 'The Revival of Pascal'. She would have had still better reason for writing that book today. Or perhaps she would have chosen the Swiss philosopher *Theophil Spoerri's* heading (1955): 'An introduction to the thought of Pascal as a philosophy for man of tomorrow'.

# IV

## On Misunderstanding Soeren Kierkegaard

When I choose to comment on misunderstanding Soeren Kierkegaard instead of on understanding him, I have three good
reasons for my choice. The first is that it sounds more exciting
and therefore appeals more to the reader's curiosity. Secondly,
if my treatment of Kierkegaard should have no sense for my
reader, this reader will have to grant me at least one point: I
have myself served as a striking illustration of my own topic.

But the third and, after all, really decisive reason, may
be observed simply from a glance at the multifarious writings
of Soeren Kierkegaard himself. Has there ever existed an author
who invited misunderstandings more liberally? He writes the
*Diary of the Seducer (Forförerens Dagbok), Christian Speeches
(Christelige Taler)* and whimsical dialectical inquiries, now this,
now that, without interruption and without a distinctive turning point, and in each of his works he performs with a never
failing mastery. Not a single unsuccessful word or a limping
illustration ever reveals him as being in a foreign field. How,
then, can we know when and where he is really himself, how can
we be sure in which way and to what extent he intends his
different writings to be taken seriously? If everything is to be
taken seriously in the same way and to the same extent, the
author himself must obviously be a person who cannot expect
to be taken seriously at all.

To this basic question Kierkegaardian research seems to have
provided at least one answer for every scholar. I say 'at least',
because in some cases students of Kierkegaard have changed their

minds after having reconsidered the problem. Certainly I find no reason to mock them for doing so; perhaps I will join their company some day — who knows? But as the number of opinions comes to at least one per interpreter, and the number of interpreters has increased by now to some hundreds, an essay on misunderstanding Soeren Kierkegaard should have a wide variety in its choice of material. However, just to review and enumerate misunderstandings of Kierkegaard would be a fairly boring task, besides being a rather useless one. So, with the clearest of consciences, I think we may leave such an enterprise aside. Far more interesting and far more instructive is an attempt to understand the misunderstandings, that is, to understand what basic possibilities of misunderstanding are really there. After having made a survey of these possibilities, I shall permit myself to trace, as a kind of conclusion, my own unassuming understanding (or misunderstanding if so it seems to the reader, just as the views of others have seemed to me).

## 1.

But what do we intend to signify by that word 'understanding'? To some people the question, no doubt, sounds so simple, not to say trivial, as to be hardly worth asking. Nevertheless it is, as a matter of fact, the basic problem of humanistic studies. Understanding a man, does that mean looking at him as far as possible the way he looks at himself? Interpreting his works, does that mean repeating their contents but in slightly different terms? Or should I bring along my own ideas of man and of the world and 'understand' him by locating him on my personal map — even if he himself would have been enraged at such treatment?

Among Kierkegaard scholars we certainly find both of these basic understandings of understanding represented. Moreover, I wonder if the contrast between the two of them ever became more manifest than in their very treatment of *Ironiens Magister*. The most clear-cut advocate of the idea of reproduction is the German professor, *Hermann Diem*, who, in a series of monographs on Kierkegaard (the first appeared in the late 1920s, the last in 1950), maintains that the only genuine interest in Kierkegaard must be in the study of his 'existential dialectic', that is, his peculiar method of dealing personally with the problems of life; and this method, he argues, can only be understood if already taken as the prescribed one for dealing with Kierkegaard's writings. Here we face an obvious *circulus interpretationis*: Kierkegaard must already show us how to study Kierkegaard; in order to understand him aright we have to deal with him in exactly the way he himself dealt with the problems of human existence.

At the opposite end we could quote scores of psychological, speculative and historico-philosophical analyses of Kierkegaard which very clearly make it their aim to 'understand' him by locating him within the frames of some doctrinal structure which the student certainly brought to his Kierkegaardian studies from elsewhere. Kierkegaard's own protest against the Hegelian doctrine of history being governed by reason, has not prevented certain interpreters from enrolling him as a necessary link in the chain of rationally motivated historical events. According to Hegel every historical phenomenon must develop its own contrast (thesis and antithesis); obviously, therefore, it is a great temptation to the heirs of Hegel to conceive Hegel as the thesis and Kierkegaard as his antithesis; the first of them being, above all, the great philosopher of community, the other the great spokesman of individuality. *Hiin Enkelte* (the individual) may very easily be reckoned as the step following *der Gemeingeist* (the corporate spirit) in the architecturally ordered stairs of historical development. In this scheme 'understanding' Kierkegaard has taken the form of seeing him as a propagator and a money collector of precisely that philosophy which his entire literary production is an attempt to chastise.

Something similar may be said of the not infrequent endeavors to explain his ideas by means of more or, especially, less successful psychological or psychoanalytical charms. Clearly, if Kierkegaard had not been lured by some of his fellow students to accompany them to a brothel sometime during his years at the university . . . or if he had not happened to peep through the keyhole of his parents' bedroom when he was five, we would have missed all this awful and futile waste of ink.

If we were to accuse those interpreters who have dispatched Kierkegaard by just adapting him into some systematic and well-arranged psychological or historico-philosophical herbarium, of misunderstanding, they would no doubt shake their heads, and in a certain sense quite justifiably. According to their own concept of understanding they have, no doubt, understood, and understood so completely as to leave no alarming or troublesome question unanswered. They have used what is for them the key to human existence, and the door has opened to them, gracefully and without difficulty. If Kierkegaard himself happened to hold a different opinion on the task and nature of understanding, then so much the worse for him. To these people the Kierkegaardian dialectics and paradoxes are but testimonies of the regular rise and fall of the waves of the Idea along the beach of history, or perhaps of the power exercised by neurosis and irresistible imagination in a spoiled mind, neither more nor less.

Of course nobody can 'prove' that these interpreters have 'misunderstood' Kierkegaard — what could such a 'proof' be? Still, when I dare to label their interpretations 'misunderstandings', it is because Kierkegaard's analysis of human existence seems to me to be relevant and meaningful in such a way that I as a human being simply have to respond to his challenge. His descriptions and judgments affect my situation in such a way that I cannot help asking, Is this true, is this man right? I cannot let his message evaporate into some misty *Weltgeist* (universal spirit) or dissolve into the activity of hormones, because this would mean shutting my ears to important things which the author himself wants to tell me, and thus not even trying to come face to face with the man himself. If we are really to take the challenge of Soeren Kierkegaard seriously, we must consider every sign that directs us away from the face-to-face encounter to be a sign that misdirects us.

But in saying this, am I not really supporting the methodological claims of Hermann Diem? I don't think so. Let me make myself clearer by adding a few comments on the position of

Diem, which can fairly be said to represent the position of the typically 'existentialist' and 'dialectical' interpretation of Kierkegaard. I cannot immediately see that it would be consistent with Kierkegaard's own claims to concentrate our attention predominantly on his 'method'. Kierkegaard himself is far from being 'existentialist' enough to let 'truth' be absorbed by some general method of seeking truth. On the contrary, as a philosopher and theologian he is to a certain extent a clear-cut dogmatist. Certainly, he has written no systematic *exposé* of Christian dogmatics. The precise dogmatic concept, however, is to him important enough. It is his spear, with which he vigorously pierces all the defensive pseudo-ideas of fugitive man, thus to dispatch every excuse and exculpation. Certainly, the brave Soeren handles this weapon brilliantly, but he is not like a performing knight who calls for our admiring attention. The point is not the handling but the hit, and, of course, the question as to whether the hit is as damaging as the assailant would have us believe. It is the contents, the message, the meaning, which is his concern, not the method in itself.

Of course, we don't get an adequate impression of Kierkegaard's message without considering how and to what extent his representation is determined by his strategy. In this sense his method must always be *a* concern of his interpreter's but not *the* concern. This we have to bear in mind when we proceed to ask the following question: In writing the way he writes — that is, in, so to say, throwing all kinds of opinions and standpoints right in the face of his reader — what is Soeren Kierkegaard's real purpose? If this or that is his message, why doesn't he tell us so quite plainly, instead of presenting his readers with lots of more or less conflicting ideas and opinions?

It should be noted that in two of his writings he has himself given account of his *Forfatterskab* (writer's production). He professes himself to be a religious author. From the very beginning his purpose has been to represent Christianity. Therefore he starts with a presentation of the aesthetical existence. This is his point of departure, from here he wants to lead his reader on and away, and at the same time he has quite consciously arranged his personal life so as to make it a supplement to his literary endeavors.

However, as a certain unsteadiness in the representation itself reveals, one should not put too much confidence in this alleged strategy. Before even having completed our picture of this grand design, Kierkegaard happens to betray the fact that sometimes he wrote at random, and that his writings were mainly determined by purely personal impulses. Not till afterwards, he tells us, when he was able to see his entire production as a coherent process, did he discover the wise plan of divine providence underlying and governing his more or less blind efforts. And if we examine his diaries, we find still more material to complicate the question. It is therefore easy to see why different Kierkegaard exegetes have arrived at opposite conclusions. Some of them praise the magnificent plan and unity of the *Forfatterskab,* others maintain that he changed his purpose or even that he held different plans and conflicting opinions at the same time. Either group has plenty of references to use in support of its conclusion — and just as many to ignore for the very same purpose.

If we want to do justice both to the unity and to the multiplicity of Kierkegaard's *Forfatterskab,* we have to admit that in his own conscious purpose and in his own attitude to his topics there is a good deal of shifting and, certainly, a never-ceasing development. But in spite of the shifting viewpoints and wavering personal interests that influence the life of Soeren Kierkegaard, a theme is to be found which definitely makes of his literary production something unitary: the relation between human existence and Christian faith, man in personal responsibility and freedom being brought to face the paradox of Christianity. The unity should not be sought in the person of the author, but in the constant focus of the issues fascinating him; not on a psychological level, but on a purely thematic one; not in the writer handling his problems, but in the problems handling him. The multitude of pseudonyms with which he disguises himself are not advocating different doctrines of existence and faith, but different alternatives of personal attitude. The pseudonyms do not reason differently — they choose differently.

If we keep this in mind, we also escape much of the dismal discussion which has been carried on about how to use the sources. While Diem, for example, has maintained that all Kierkegaard's writings deserve the same amount of attention, with the pseudonyms serving a necessary purpose within the full dialectical structure, the majority of interpreters have been inclined to locate Kierkegaard's personal concept of life in his edifying (non-pseudonymous) writings, considering the aesthetical and philosophical productions (pseudonymous) a more or less incidental pastime. The diaries have been evaluated by some as the basic material for studying Kierkegaard — because they allegedly give us the keys to his most secret rooms. Others have pushed the diaries aside, because they obviously suffer from shifting humors and fluctuating sentiments.

These problems, too, are dismissed as soon as we turn away from questions of Kierkegaard's personal moods, experiences and impressions, to search for the concept of reality which his multifarious *Forfatterskab* constantly reflects. As far as I can see, Kierkegaard must have come, at least around New Year 1842-43, to a relatively explicit understanding of the 'categories' with which man is confronted by his 'existence'.


2.


Man and Christianity — that is his theme. And obviously the relation between 'Christian' and 'human' is presented in his works in two seemingly contrasting ways. Now correspondence and understanding, now rivalry and conflict are emphasized. On the one hand we are introduced to 'subjectivity is the truth', the responsibility of the individual, the pain of choice and the act of freedom — and all this, the essential privilege of human existence, seems to find its fulfillment and its most ardent expression exactly in Christian faith. On the other hand Christianity is presented as 'the paradox', it is said to be contrary to reason; facing 'the possibility of offense' *(Forargelsens Mulighed)* man has to admit as an historical fact that eighteen hundred years ago God walked in our streets and our lanes, looking exactly like the rest of us, and to accept the judgment which this fact passes upon us all: we needed such a really extraordinary event in order to be delivered from our falsity and corruption. Is Christianity the crown of human existence or its annihilation? This apparent ambiguity leads us to the very core of the Kierkegaardian problem. If we manage to understand its meaning, we have understood Soeren Kierkegaard.

Like all other problems in the world, this one is most easily solved by those who never discovered it. And they are quite a few. I think of the commentators who overlooked either one or the other of the two sides of Kierkegaard's determination of the relation 'Christian'/'human', some, perhaps, due to a limited study of his writings, others due to a fancy for some particular aspect which radiated such a charm that all others faded behind it. In this way we have got, among others, the well-known tradition of interpreting Kierkegaard as a pietistic preacher, a fervid spokesman for the 'inner-mission' type of low-church revivalism. Or we have frequently seen him portrayed as the stern prophet of individualism and subjectivism, whom only the aftereffects of a depraving education could prevent from completely dethroning God. Of these two pictures the first is undoubtedly the more harmless, because it has usually been launched with very little scholarly pretension. It is a more serious case that men like Georg Brandes, Torgny Segerstedt and Anathon Aall — just to mention an advocate from each of the three Scandinavian countries — have contributed to the formation of prejudices which still exercise their influence in fairly well educated circles.

A relatively simple solution can also be attained if the apparent contrasts are sufficiently spiritualized. If we picture Kierkegaard as a 'mystic' in the traditional sense, the self-contradiction also fades. The 'paradox' and the 'offense' may then be conceived as symbols of obstacles man has to overcome in order to penetrate to the depths of his own being — and, suddenly, the 'subjectivity' and the 'paradox' are heartily reconciled. Quite a few interpreters have chosen this track, but with different degrees of persistency and consequence. In support of this view Kierkegaard's relatively thorough occupation with some of the Medieval mystics may be referred to, and early nineteenth-century Romanticism has offered a suitable historical background. But on Romanticism as well as on mysticism Kierkegaard's own observations are very critical. After all, his paradox cannot be reduced to something merely psychological; the historical fact as such is a constitutive part of it. If the crucial point was not an historical event, but some religious idea or some psychological scheme, then the matter would not be a 'paradox' according to Kierkegaard's terminology.

In recent years it has become more and more generally realized that Kierkegaard does not belong to what may, not very precisely, be called 'the mystical tradition'. The mystical part of the interpretation of Kierkegaard has been superseded more and more by the different 'existential' types. A certain historical line combining Kierkegaard and modern existentialism cannot be denied. Both he and it condemn the tendency to inspect the riddles of life impersonally and 'neutrally'; death to the thinker who pretends to have understood everything but does not understand himself! So far existential philosophy is undisputedly Kierkegaard's legitimate heir. But somewhat more dubious is that interpretation which sees him only as a precursor of modern existentialism, or which finds the key for analyzing him in some form of it.

A distinctive example of such an interpretation of Kierkegaard we find in Johannes Slök's *Die Antropologie Kierkegaards* (Copenhagen 1954), in many respects an excellent piece of work which makes a number of striking observations. But even in Slök's exegesis the tension between the two poles in Kierkegaard's thought is efficiently eliminated, by means of a dexterous little trick of mediation. To Slök the key is not at all some mystical experience of the deity, but the present instant *(Öjebliket)* and the existential freedom of choice. Faith is something which man does not 'possess' but into which he has to enter by choice again and again. But in this very choice man fulfills his basic human task. Faith is the definite expression of human existence as a free commitment to life in its inescapable state of departure, and at the same time it is the most radical offense to acquisitive man — and who of us is not acquisitive? In this way the Gospel becomes as well a 'yes' as a 'no' to 'natural' man, depending upon which man or, rather, which attitude of man we choose to label 'natural'. Christianity as the definite 'yes' to human existence must, of course, be the most radical 'no' to all attempts at establishing a non-existential humanity.

But even about this existentialized Kierkegaard we must say as we did about the mysticized one: the 'paradox' has actually been pushed aside, the basic omission of the historical event and the corresponding exaltation of a general attitude (psychological or dialectical; in this connection the choice does not matter) is unmistakable enough. And, thus, the very 'possibility of offense', and the subjective passion of existence have been transformed several thousand volts down. Most existentialist interpreters of Kierkegaard have suffered from an unshakeable belief in having found a scheme which cannot fail to grasp the core of existence and of everything in this world which is worth grasping, and either Kierkegaard must be their man or — well, that is an alternative they have wisely left aside.

From all this a slight impression should remain of the dangers involved in making some familiar and comparatively simple philosophical idea the principle for interpreting Kierkegaard. Up to this day such endeavors have born very impressive but not very convincing fruit. Kierkegaard is no more 'the last Viking' of romanticism than a 'John the Baptist' of modern existentialism. From whichever side you attack his position, there will always remain something which remains especially his own. Before I, the interpreter, can judge him according to my own presuppositions, I must first listen to him admitting his own. Finally, of course, I have also to judge his presuppositions in choosing my own, but I cannot uncritically assume I have identified them and argue as if mine were his.

There still remains a theory, which has been frequently advocated by students of Kierkegaard, and which needs a short comment. I mean the various assertions about some irreconciled duality in Kierkegaard's own basic attitude toward his problems. The most outstanding spokesman of such an idea, the late Swedish bishop Torsten Bohlin, developed his view in a long series of monographs on Kierkegaard: *there* Kierkegaard's personal faith sparkles, his experience of a profound security and harmony derived from the presence of God in the believing soul, *there* his philosophy of the paradox towers up without any organic contact whatsoever with the said faith as just a sad product of his intellectual enslavement in Hegelian dialecticism and Medieval dogmaticism. In other words, there exists a basic controversy between Kierkegaard the edifying preacher and Kierkegaard (or rather Victor Eremita, Johannes de silentio, Johannes Climacus, Nicolaus Notabene, Hilarius Bogbinder, H. H. and Anti-Climacus) the dialectical philosopher and theologian. The answer to this claim is that such a basic lack of consistency is hard to imagine in a thinker as single-minded in his quest for consistency as he was adept at achieving it. And if we undertake to examine his writings piece by piece, we soon find that this dualism between preacher and dialectician must be a fiction. Where is the dialectician, for example, more vividly alive than in the edifying pamphlet *Kjerlighedens Gjerninger* (Acts of Love)? And where is the personal passion of faith more ardent than in *Indövelse i Christendom* (Training in Christianity), the main plea for the 'paradox' and the 'offense'?

The result of these excursions in different directions seems obvious: the ambiguity in Kierkegaard's description of the relation between Humanity and Christianity cannot be considered either unconscious or involuntary any more than it can be removed by symbolizing or existentializing it. The ambiguity — or should we rather say, the duality — is his proper concern.

### 3.

Let me then, finally, give a sketch, as brief and as simplified as possible, of how, in my opinion, this duality must be understood.

Man, says Kierkegaard, is a synthesis of 'time' and 'eternity'. This is in itself by no means a new postulate; many voices, from the time of classical Antiquity, have maintained the same postulate. But Kierkegaard parts company with his classical precursors in emphasizing the synthesis itself as an ethical task. That is, he rejects the one-sided cult of the 'eternal', nonmaterial component, so characteristic of all traditional 'idealism'. To Platonism and all its offspring separation of the two natures of man is the great aim; his spiritual, eternal nature ought to be delivered from its imprisonment in a temporal, material body subject to change and decay. But according to Kierkegaard it is not separation and flight from our material nature, but synthesis involving a positive relation to existence here and now that is the meaning and task of life. The *synthesis* is our task. But note the word 'task'; the synthesis is our *task*, always our *task*. Life never becomes a complete and fulfilled something, which we can enjoy inspecting. Our destiny always towers in front of us. Man is not a given entity, something ready and finished; he 'becomes himself' only by choosing himself — choosing, not *having chosen*.

So the point is to grasp freedom: the pain and the bliss implicit in my double orientation, every moment being in the stream of time *and* in eternity. To lose sight of eternity is easy enough. To mount to it on the wings of illusion, forgetting one's own existence in *Timeligheden* (temporality), is likewise fairly easy. But to possess eternity without shutting one's eyes for a single moment and without turning away from oneself or from one's situation in time — that is not possible without faith, that presupposes decision and passion. That is existence, that is my acceptance of my own basic condition as a human being.

To man wholeheartedly engaged in this task of existence, Christianity asserts its unpleasant claim: 'you cannot but fail without me'. If man has forgotten his existential task, Christianity simply makes no sense. The same view was strongly advocated by Kierkegaard's great compatriot and contemporary Grundtvig; in spite of the contempt the former usually showed for the *Brageskjald* (the poet of Brage), they agree in the claim: *Menneske först og Christen saa!* (First be a man, a Christian next!). Where the task and the responsibility are disposed of and the subjectivity and the passion have faded away, Christianity is reduced to sweet and nauseous talk. This is obviously the reason why Kierkegaard pushes a series of *Stadier* (stages) in between the unreflecting mode of life and Christianity. Christian faith cannot be reduced to a mimicking of certain phrases, it is not a ripe fruit falling into the hat of some sleeping idler. The sacred words are not sacred any more when they are recited outside their proper 'situation'. Only 'the person situated in the extreme of existence' *(den i Existentsens Yderste Bestedte)* is able to understand and grasp the concern of Christianity.

And here we touch at the real positive link which for Kierkegaard connects human and Christian existence. It is the passion of personal engagement, of being situated in the 'instant', the crossroads of time and eternity, of never escaping the responsibility of a choice. It is the basic condition of human existence itself. And just in accepting this condition, man is led to come face to face with Christianity. In his description of this meeting it may be seen how completely his concept of Christianity parts company with those of Pietism and Mysticism. To him the point of conversion is not an advance from one state — or stage — or psychological condition, to another. The essential thing is not a kind of continuous progress, nor of mental change taking place once for all. Even within Christianity 'subjectivity' remains the truth, and every flight from this truth is predestined to end up in hypocrisy. No emotional experience and no rational calculus can grant me the assurance needed. I can find no objective guarantee whatever. This causes the tension, and the pain which is inseparable from a human existence that is true to itself. Also, a Christian, in this sense, exists in his humanity; in fact such a Christian is the only human being who has consistently been confronted with the meaning of human existence and consciously made it his choice.

Christianity does not leave it to man himself to locate the true and redemptive unity of time and eternity wherever it might please him. It points at one definite historical person and maintains that only in him are time and eternity really linked together and that only in commitment to him can a human being ever reach a true synthesis of temporal and eternal. Through this claim Christianity actually intensifies the human *Existentslidenskap* (passion of existence), increases the affliction of decision and aggravates the pain of freedom. It becomes the supreme expression of humanity, of freedom defying the general outlook of the spectator and mocking the 'professor' who has made himself an impersonal nonentity, an anonymous part of some universal 'system'. Christianity is the definite expression of humanity.

So far our reproductive sketch differs little from some of the existentialist interpretations of Kierkegaard. In proceeding to a description of the 'offensive' character of Christianity, however, we must leave these allies behind. The offense of Christianity consists basically in its accusation against man, 'Thou art not in the truth!' The belief in Christ is inseparable from the consciousness of being, in oneself, a helpless prey to falsity. If man in any way possessed truth within himself, if, by any means, it was sufficient to develop something already at his disposal, the belief in a incarnate God would be meaningless and, at the same time, existentially completely insignificant. The incarnation can only become meaningful to me if I know that I do not possess truth but need to receive it as a gift from outside my own reach.

The dogmas of the 'God-man' and of a general human corruption are, as clearly seen in the *Philosophical Fragments,* inseparable from one another; and in their mutual dependency they are simply constitutive of Christianity. If they are omitted, we remain with Socrates: man himself is the depository of truth, and 'revelation' is basically excluded. The interpretation of human existence involved in the Christian doctrine of salvation is this: not only unexistential man, who hides himself in some impersonal collective 'the multitude' 'the system', 'the general opinion', or in some such (just as impersonal) aesthetical superlative as 'the matchless', 'the most wonderful', 'the truly most impressive and wonderful' etc., but even man who is seriously concerned with his existence, is unable to break the dominion of falsity. Just when he is most earnestly engaged in seeking the truth, man is hit by the challenge of Christianity and thus driven to 'the most extreme edge of choice': either believe in Christ or turn in holy anger against this offensive attack on the noble pretensions of your most sacred endeavors.

'Subjectivity is the truth' and 'Subjectivity is the untruth'; these seemingly contradictory statements in *Concluding Unscientific Postscript* are, of course, put beside each other for some purpose — the author hasn't simply lost his own track from one chapter to the next. The connection between the two postulates, in my opinion, can only be as follows. It is necessary that man be driven away from every hiding place of impersonal and improper existence and forced to count only his own responsibility and his own possibilities, in order to discover that even his best efforts don't suffice for establishing a contact with God, without which contact there is not even a contact with human destiny. Subjectivity, the full consciousness of being left alone in my own responsibility where no pawnbroker in this world can provide me with a single penny, is the only human attitude open to truth. Therefore the aim of Christianity is least of all to help men out of this embarrassment. To Christianity subjectivity is a much beloved and most helpful ally. But there is one important circumstance which must be underlined. Subjectivity is an open attitude; it cannot turn around in self-inspection and self-admiration, and thus make a closed sphere. In doing so, it would objectify itself, which *per definitionem* would be to make itself something non-subjective: that is, subjectivity would no more be subjectivity, only some specific kind of objectivity. Here Kierkegaard's concern differs radically from that of all the ideologies usually listed in the large school of 'subjectivism'. 'Subjectivism' itself is neither more nor less than a kind of 'objectivism', making subjectivity an object, a theory, a competitor to other systems claiming universal validity. Anyone saying, 'I see a subject', is wrong — provided that the word is meant in its grammatical and philosophical sense. I, as the subject of my own visual act, can only see an object. And if I maintain, 'I see myself,' this 'I' and this 'myself' are by no means identical. 'I' is the subject of the act, 'myself' the object.

In his concept of subjectivity Kierkegaard has, in contrast

to traditional 'subjectivism', fully realized and expressed this point. Subjectivity is no theory of man and truth, but an attitude; subjectivity is existence not trying to hide from itself. If humanity finishes up in some theory of humanity without distinguishing between matter and theory, humanity is lost — it has been 'thingified' and listed among other 'things'. Thus, in becoming something completed and definite, in establishing itself as a new system, subjectivity, the truth, does away with itself and becomes subjectivity, the untruth.

The discovery of this untruth is inescapable in the face of Christianity. True subjectivity knows that it is not a depository of truth but an attitude tending toward truth. But in actual life this true subjectivity is never a possession, and, unfortunately, man is always making himself a possessor; he even claims subjectivity as his own property. In pretending to make himself master of truth, man thus makes himself master of a corrupted existence.

Subjectivity thus becomes ambiguous, in the daily existence of sinful man (i. e. man making himself master of something which, as a property, does not rightfully belong to him) true existence may to a certain extent become a directive aim, but its dominion never becomes undisputed. Man, faithful to his existence, may discover this, and proceed from the experience of subjectivity as truth toward the complementary experience of 'subjectivity' as falsity. But Christianity alone grants a full cognition of the duplicity.

Thus the 'God-man' pretending to bring man the full and only redemptive truth, has human subjectivity as an ally and as an enemy at the same time. If subjectivity were nothing but subjectivity, it would not engage in a conflict with the understanding of truth as a gift being brought to man from outside by a special divine messenger. On the contrary, it would find such a postulate coinciding with and reaffirming its own cognition and endeavors. But the actual duplex state of subjectivity must necessarily cause a duplex relation between Christianity and human existence, a 'yes' and a 'no', which cannot be separated from each other. The Christian belief in Christ is the true fulfillment of human destiny *and* the protest that most offends against the belief in human self-sufficiency. And it contains the claim that this sufficiency is always there — hidden or manifest — and that only confrontation with Christ grants the truth because it grants the full unveilment.

With all his dialectical ability Kierkegaard attacks the problem from ever new angles. The reader is never allowed to settle down, either in a dogmatical or in an 'undogmatical' type of dogmatism. Existence and faith both consist in departure, and departure in this case means repeated return to an interminable movement. But this movement itself is, like all movements, a movement in relation to something fixed and stable. To Kierkegaard this stable point is not something within individual man himself; it belongs exclusively to God, over whom man can never acquire dominion because God is always claiming dominion over man.

Those who happen to understand this, have automatically understood the concern of Kierkegaard. And those who have heard God's claim of dominion as a claim directed to themselves personally, have understood him the way he wants to be understood. His legitimate heir is not the writer or the scholar winning laurels for admirable presentation of his genius or extravaganza but *hiin Enkelte* (the individual) who, in 'fear and trembling', consents to being led on from the problem of Kierkegaard to the problem of himself. That is where every reader of Kierkegaard will finish up — unless he has very definitely misunderstood the master.

# V

## Kierkegaard's 'Paradox'

*A Sketch of its Meaning, with Reference to some Traditional
Applications of the Term*

In the minds of many persons who otherwise know very little
about Soeren Kierkegaard, there are at least two notions that
are closely associated with his name, those of 'the individual'
*(hiin Enkelte)* and 'the paradox'. These ideas, both of which are
so characteristic of the thought of the great philosopher, express
a task and a difficulty set for a human being. Man's destiny is
to become 'an individual', and 'the paradox' constitutes the
challenge and the question he has got to hear and respond to.
His immediate thought is to flee from the demand of 'individuality' and hide in the multitude; from the confrontation with
'the paradox' he tries to escape through the gate of 'objectivity'.
Instead of listening to God's demand of him and responding
in 'fear and trembling', he is always disposed to react on behalf
of his 'most venerable contemporaries'. From this it may be
understood that to be 'an individual' and to believe in 'the
paradox' are not entirely different tasks. Although the categories may occur in somewhat different contexts, and the term
'individuality' seems to have a wider application (it is found
also in connections where the religious bearing of the problems
is not mentioned), the two categories referred to are inseparably
linked together. No one can ever become an 'individual' except
by accepting 'the paradox' of the eternal God who is concerned
with his individual and temporal life, and no one can believe
this 'paradox' unless he has experienced himself to be 'the
individual', unable to hide anywhere or behind anyone. Obvi-

ously, therefore, to be concerned with one of these categories is not so much to be concerned with a part of the Kierkegaardian philosophy as to be occupied with it as a whole.

1.

It may be useful to bear the above in mind when we undertake to examine Kierkegaard's conception of 'the paradox'. The presence of this term within the Kierkegaardian writings is not to be regarded as a multitude of solitary islands in an ocean, nor as a sharply circumscribed county within a country. The term stands in a context; in fact it itself constitutes the context.

As we try to understand Kierkegaard's paradox we should also keep in mind two other contexts which are very important: the historical context by which Kierkegaard himself might have been influenced, and the still more obvious historical context in which we place ourselves as Kierkegaard's interpreters. When Kierkegaard uses the term 'paradox', he is not handling a creation of his own, and, when we ask what he means by 'paradox', we are not the first to make the inquiry. Before we consider the function of the term in Kierkegaard's own writings, we shall very briefly note the history of the term, and also its history within the Kierkegaard-interpretations.

As far as I can see, most of the traditional concepts of 'paradox' may be said to belong to one of two main classes. The Greek combination, *para-doxon* (being beside reason), may be understood in the way of the Latin expression *contra rationem*, against reason, or in the way of *super rationem*, beyond reason. In either case the maintenance of the paradox will signify opposition to a rationalistic attitude, i. e. to any immediate supposition of reason as an adequate key to the riddles of life. The paradox of the first class will seek to defeat rationalism by means of its own weapons. As its final consequence it will lead to the conclusion of Tertullian: *credo quia absurdum*, it is true because it is impossible. The common rules of logic will be substituted by the dialectic of the double truth. What is true in an ethical or religious setting may, or even must, be wrong in a scientific one. On the other hand, the paradox of the second class will not fight reason with reason's own weapons, but escapes the battlefield, the sooner the better. In its consistent form it will express the intellectual attitude of mysticism. It will be the paradox of a Sebastian Franck: the turning away from the outward world to the experiences of the 'soul' as the one and only important reality. Typical in this connection is Schleiermacher's definition of religion as *weder ein Wissen noch ein Thun,* neither understanding nor acting (the German wording is not adequately covered by the English), but a form of immediate self-consciousness, a feeling of unconditioned dependency. Schleiermacher himself does not use the word 'paradox', and it would scarcely have fitted into his philosophical terminology at all. Nevertheless, his *weder ein Wissen*... very directly expresses the *para-doxon,* and his whole philosophy of religion is a classical paradigm of paradox, not at all in the sense of conflict, but definitely in that of a total difference between belief and theoretical knowledge. It is a rather natural thing to mention Schleiermacher, since most of nineteenth-century continental philosophy in the fields of religion and ethics has been so fundamentally dependent upon him, and a great number of interpreters have also tried to show that Kierkegaard belonged to this Schleiermacherian tradition.

As a whole, Kierkegaard's paradox has been understood along the traditional lines, and the main topic of discussion among his interpreters has been whether 'the paradox' stands for belief *against* reason or for belief *beyond* reason. Has orthodoxy combined with his fancy for abstract dialectics and his attempts to defeat Hegelianism, and thus driven him into the arms of the *credo quia absurdum*? Or, has his abhorrence of 'objectivism' and intellectualism, and his suspicion of 'doctrine' led him into the company of the nineteenth-century *Erlebnis*-theologians? For instance, according to H. R. Mackintosh, Christ as the paradox of Kierkegaard 'is constituted by sheer essential contradiction', while A. Bärthold finds the paradox to mean 'that theology has to lead on from thought to a personal conception of life.'

In this connection it is very instructive to compare two of the most important interpreters of Kierkegaard in this generation, Torsten Bohlin and Emanuel Hirsch. Both of these outstanding theologians may be classified as belonging to the Schleiermacherian tradition, and both interpret Kierkegaard as a theologian to whom the personal religious experience is the real issue. Neither of them is in doubt that in him they find a fellow believer. But concerning the paradox they are unable to agree. To Hirsch, the paradox seems to be the definite affirmation of Kierkegaard's anti-intellectualistic religiosity. According to Bohlin, there is a deplorable inconsistency between Kierkegaard's personal faith and his paradoxical dialecticism.

Bohlin comes to the conclusion that there are two 'differing lines in Kierkegaard's dogmatic thinking'. The first is mainly predominant in the edifying writings, as well as in *The Concept of Dread* and in *The Sickness unto Death*; the second is particularly found in *Philosophical Fragments, Postscript,* and *Training in Christianity*. The first line is dominated by a personal experience of sin and grace, the second by the theory of Christ as the absolute paradox. According to Bohlin the paradox does not have its source in Kierkegaard's personal faith but in the 'Hellenistic-Socratic distinction between time and eternity, presuming these to be of infinitely different qualities, which has in his [Kierkegaard's] thinking established an alliance with Augustine's doctrine of human nature as being totally corrupted by sin'. His theory of the two 'lines' found very wide acceptance among interpreters of Kierkegaard some twenty or thirty years ago, but has later constantly been losing in influence. In many cases, however, the theory seems to have been rejected without a serious test.

Emanuel Hirsch, whose early presentation of Kierkegaard is not unlike that of Torsten Bohlin, has through a further study of Kierkegaard been brought to a somewhat altered conclusion. In his *Kierkegaard-Studien* he maintains that the paradox is not governed by a dialectical or a dogmatic interest, but that it intends to protect the purity of personal religious experience from any intrusion on the part of non-religious spiritual factors. It advocates a conception of faith, not unlike that of the Medieval mystics. To understand the structure of Kierkegaard's thought is to understand that this kind of a paradox is the farewell to any type of intellectualism in the realm of ethics and religion. We find this same conception expressed very distinctly by Eduard Geismar: 'No dogmatic formula can express faith. This is what Kierkegaard wants to secure by the doctrine of the paradox. There can be no dogmatic conception of this paradox'.

Bohlin or Hirsch, against or beyond reason — which interpretation of Kierkegaard's paradox is the correct one? Or, is there perhaps a third possibility? These are the questions we shall have to bear in mind when we proceed to analyze a few of the more characteristic among Kierkegaard's own pronouncements in this field.

2.

Let us begin by examining the writings of the pseudonymous Johannes Climacus, which are the works in which the term is most frequently used. In *Philosophical Fragments* the term 'paradox' is used in a rather ambiguous way. However, its function within the context of the book as a whole seems clear enough. According to Socrates, truth can never be the object of teaching or learning. All cognition is in principle recollection. Truth is an 'eternal' possession of man, and the importance of any teacher and of any actual historical moment is reduced to being that of the 'occasion'. No man can give another man the truth; he can only instigate him to seek it within himself. The problem of the *Fragments* is, What would be the consequences if, in order to transcend this Socratic conception, we should postulate an historical origin of man's consciousness of the eternal? In such a conception man must not be assumed to possess the essential truth beforehand; he is not holding in his hand the key to his own riddle. But in one concrete historical moment he receives the truth, which until that moment was not his. Such an acceptance of the truth must again be subject to the meeting with, and consequently also to the existence of, a teacher who possesses the truth. Such a teacher can be none other than 'the God in time'. This is the paradox. 'If we posit the moment, then the paradox is there; for in its most abbreviated form the paradox may be called the moment; by means of the moment the pupil becomes untruth; man, who knew himself, instead of self-knowledge gets the consciousness of sin etc. As soon as we only assume the moment, everything else follows.'

But in the chapter 'The Absolute Paradox', we find the term paradox also used in another manner. The author does a rather astonishing thing. For a while he leaves his argument, and instead of continuing his hypothetical experiment, he reasons from an empirical basis. Thought, like any other passion, wills its own annihilation. In its 'paradoxical' passion reason seeks a collision with an unknown and unknowable reality, because such a collision would grant the only possibility of the fulfillment of its desire. This is 'the highest paradox of thought', reason wanting to do away with itself, which again is identical with giving itself up to the absolutely unknowable reality. This reality Climacus chooses to call 'the God'. There can be no event more happy than the collision between paradox and reason in the decisive moment of mutual understanding. But we note an ambiguous use of the term 'paradox', and conclude that the combination of the empirical 'paradoxicality' of thought as a function and the hypothetical 'paradox' of God as an historical being is problematical in this chapter, and from a logical point of view rather unsatisfactory.

On the whole, however, the meaning of 'paradox' in *Fragments* is clear. The paradox is 'the God in time' and that understanding of human existence which is inseparably linked together with this fact. The positive relation between reason and paradox suggested in the description of the paradoxical structure of thought seems in a way explained through the double conception of the terms 'history' and 'faith' as set forth in the chapter, 'Interlude'. But in order to find the full and satisfactory explanation of the ambiguity of the concept of the paradox, we have to proceed to the treatment of this term as it is found in *Concluding Unscientific Postscript to the Philosophical Fragments*.

In this work Socrates is used a little differently from the manner in which he is used in *Fragments*. In *Fragments* he is represented as the contrast to Christianity. In *Postscript* he is not primarily a contrast but an ally. Here the 'Socratic' paradox occurs as a preparation for, and as included in, the Christian paradox. Like Christianity, Socrates is an adversary of objective speculation. The 'objective' thinker identifies his own thoughts with the eternal truth, and thus leaves himself and his own existence in time out of consideration. He imagines himself encircled by proofs and guarantees, eternity is his secure possession. His thinking involves him in no personal risk whatever. Socrates, on the other hand, understands that to 'existing' man the eternal can never be an object of static and secure possession. The positive relationship between existence and the eternal contains a contradiction. However, the eternal itself contains no contradiction, only the fact of its being related to an existing individual. The quintessence of the existential Socratic conception of truth must therefore be that 'objective uncertainty, held fast in the adoption of the most passionate inwardness, is the truth, the highest truth attainable for an existing person'. This again means that truth, objectively defined, must be the 'paradox'. It follows that 'subjectivity is the truth', because the objective fact can be known as nothing more than a challenge requiring a personal decision. The objective paradox requires a subjective passion as the condition for its adoption.

Johannes Climacus maintains that in Christianity this conception of truth is expressed in a still more decisive way in the assumption that 'subjectivity is the untruth'. Thus the entire problem of existence is raised anew. This does not at all mean the superseding by the new maxim of the former maxim of subjectivity being the truth. On the contrary, it is affirmed. Existence has 'marked' the existing individual a second time, and the retreat by way of objective speculation, back to the eternal, is definitely barred. In this way the 'paradox is becoming more and more apparent'.

The relation between the 'Socratic paradox' and the *paradox sensu strictiori* (the Christian paradox) is clearly expressed in a statement like this: 'The remission of sin is paradoxical in the Socratic sense, as far as the eternal truth has a reference to an existing individual, and *sensu strictiori* because the existing individual is a sinner, and through this determination existence has been marked a second time, because it will be an eternal decision within time, with retrogressive power to suspend the past, and because it depends upon the fact that God has existed in time'. The difference between the two 'paradoxes' corresponds to the difference between 'religiosity A' and 'paradoxical religiosity' as presented in the section, 'The Problem of the Fragments': 'For speculation existence has disappeared and only the pure essence is. For religiosity A only the actuality of existence is, but the eternal, however, is always concealed in it, and is present in its concealment. The paradoxical religiosity declares the opposition between existence and the eternal to be absolute . . . In the paradoxical religiosity the eternal is sought in a restricted place, and this is just the break with immanence.' The paradoxical religiosity is defined as ' "the sphere of faith". It is all to be believed against reason'.

We notice that the term 'paradox' in the Climacian writings expresses a peculiar ambiguity in the relation between Christianity and humanity. In its assumption of the exclusive historical origin of the eternal truth, Christianity enters into an unconditional conflict with any non-Christian understanding of human existence. On the other hand, the subjective passion of faith, required by 'that fact' (*hiint Faktum*, namely, the God in time) is in itself not essentially different from the passion of any other existential relation to the eternal, but just the fulfillment and the perfection of it, affirming it through adopting it as its own 'pathetic' element. Subjectivity is at the same time both the truth and the untruth. In our conclusions we shall return to this ambiguity, which we have not as yet been able fully to explain.

In the Anti-Climacian writings, *The Sickness unto Death* and *Training in Christianity*, the ambiguity will not be found. Here Christianity is exclusively regarded as a stumbling-block to natural man, and no correspondence between Christian faith and the structure of human existence is really considered. In

*The Sickness* the term 'paradox' occurs closely connected with the concept of sin. According to Christianity the antithesis of sin is not virtue, but faith. To this statement there is the following comment: 'As the foundation of this antithesis is the decisive clue of Christianity, namely, before God; and this definition again carries the decisive criterion of Christianity: the absurd, the paradox, the possibility of offense ... that an individual man should have the reality of existing before God as an *individual* man, and in consequence, that God should be concerned with the sin of man.' 'Paradox, faith, and dogma' are allies in defining sin as a positive fact of which man can only become aware through a revelation. Thus any kind of human speculation is excluded. It is not difficult to discover the principal harmony between this paradoxical conception of sin and the anthropology of the Climacian writings: truth is not the possession of man, subjectivity is the untruth. Nor is it difficult to find a trend which connects the concept of the paradox which we meet in *Training* and the essence of the Climacian writings: The rejection of the general tendency to transform Christ from an historical fact into an idea. 'He is the paradox, that history can never digest nor transform by means of a general syllogism.' The same tendency clearly dominates the two smaller 'ethical-religious essays' under the pseudonym H. H.

It is quite obvious that among the statements we have noticed, there are those which seem to support the *contra rationem* conception of the paradox, as well as others which seem to advocate a *supra rationem* view. But we can also discern an inner connection between all these seemingly disagreeing pronouncements. In either case the paradox is in some sense related to man in his totality. The paradox does not primarily occur as conflicting with one restricted function of man's spiritual life, nor as advocating a divorce between faith and certain human functions with its consequent engagement to certain others. For example, if we compare the use of the term in the Climacian writings with its use in *The Sickness* (and the Climacian writings and *The Sickness* are, indeed, very different in their whole form and composition. According to Bohlin each represents one of the two conflicting 'lines' in Kierkegaard's thought.), we find the paradox in either case closely related to the conception of 'existence'. According to Climacus the entire existence of man is marked by the fact that truth is not a possibility given to his immediate disposal. In *The Sickness* existence occurs as a task imposed upon man: the establishment in his own daily life of a synthesis of freedom and necessity; his failing aptitude for the discharging of this duty, his distress, which is his resigned staying in the unfulfilled duty, is his guilt before God, his sin, of which he cannot become aware unless informed through a revelation. In the first case, the paradox is that man does not have the eternal truth at his disposal, hence his dependency on a historical origin of the truth, either in the Socratic sense — the origin being his own personal decision — or in the Christian sense *(sensus strictior)* — the origin being his own personal decision to believe the sole and historical origin of the eternal truth. In the second case, the paradox stands for man's sin as a matter of God's concern, and consequently as a problem man can neither be aware of nor solve without an historical revelation of the eternal God. The fundamental consistency between these two conceptions should need no further demonstration.

It is not difficult to see how the Climacian contraposition of time and eternity, when considered apart from the existing man, may lead to the conception of Kierkegaard's paradox as a contrarational constellation of abstract contradictions. Nor is it hard to understand how the definition of the paradox in *The Sickness* as the sin of the individual man being God's concern, when separated from the thought of sin as a matter of existence (i. e., as a fact attached to man as a totality, of which man himself is not even able to be aware unless he is enlightened by a revelation), may be understood as representative of a suprarational religiosity. However, none of these views can be right. None of them leaves room for the function of the term 'paradox' in either context. And a principal inconsistency here would be hard to conceive of when we keep in mind Kierkegaard's dialectical genius.

In fact the Climacian writings employ the terminology of believing against reason. But the whole context indicates that 'reason' here is meant in a sense quite different from the one usual in philosophy as well as in everyday conversation. 'Reason' stands for 'objectivity', which again is the non-existential attitude of self-objectification. The subjectivity required does not mean a flight from the guarantee of reason to, for instance, the guarantee of some emotional experience, which would have been just as much of an objectification. Subjectivity means belief in a fact, of which there is no other guarantee than the fact giving itself up to me in the meeting of the decisive 'moment'. There is no part of me which I can point out as more or less related to God than any other. And here reason stands in no class of its own. Neither is reason the power bringing me to God, nor is it the enemy separating me from him. The primary concern of the paradox is not reason, but I, the existing I, the individual entirely separated from God and entirely loved by God.

3.

Thus the term 'paradox' has as its principle function the defining of the relation between Christianity and human existence, and the ambiguity of its use seems to indicate an ambiguity within this relation. We find between these two entities at the same time a fundamental correspondence and a radical discontinuity. As an existing man I have the task imposed upon me of realizing my individual existence as a synthesis of time and eternity. Christianity means continuity, because it affirms this task; and it means discontinuity, because it denies my ability to perform it, and because it consequently claims recognition as the only possible origin of my 'eternal consciousness'.

I meet this claim only in so far as I am subjectively engaged in existing. I am not called upon to acknowledge a judgment upon a condition I have in principle left behind me, but just a judgment on the existence which is my own self, and which I, even as a Christian, am bound to as my inescapable condition. Subjectivity is the truth, and the same subjectivity is the untruth. The spiritual attitude of conscious existence, the passionate tension of utter concern with the own self, and with time and eternity as its stipulating elements, is in itself the same outside Christianity as within it. Only the origin of truth itself has been moved from the attitude to the fact of an incarnation that requires the attitude. The Socratic Paradox has contributed to the constitution of the paradox *sensu eminentiori*. But, as *Fragments* already made clear, there is a decisive difference between the Socratic and the Christian conception of truth, and the transition from the former to the latter involves a determined break with immanence.

With such a view of existence Kierkegaard has laid the foundation for a conception of the paradox which is quite different from the traditional ones. The many attempts to understand him on the background of the question, Against or beyond reason?, must all be reckoned as in vain. His paradox is not primarily determined by reason, but by existence, and there is no definite either/or as to continuity and discontinuity. Or, it would be more correct to say, there is a definite either/or, and a just as definite both/and, which cannot be abstracted from one another. God is the condition, i. e. the *conditor,* of human existence, and no one can escape him; this is the reason for the continuity. God is the inaccessible, whom no man can grasp or make himself master of; this is the reason for the discontinuity. One of these two statements must not be taken to exclude the other, which might easily be done if it were isolated as an abstract principle; this is the reason for the both/and. The recognition of the former fact does not in itself include the recognition of the latter; this is the reason for the either/or: either remain with Socrates or go on to Christ. This view cannot satisfactorily be characterized as intellectualism nor as anti-intellectualism. It should rather be called existentialism and anti-existentialism in a dialectical combination, a combination which is ultimately determined by genuine Christian motives originating in the conception of faith which characterized the Reformation.

※

For documentation and further discussion of Kierkegaard's conception of the paradox the reader is referred to my book, *Samtidighedens Situation, en studie i Søren Kierkegaards kristendomsforståelse,* Oslo 1954, pp. 118-54.

# VI

## Nietzsche and Christianity

Friedrich Wilhelm Nietzsche, son of a Lutheran minister and brought up in solid ecclesiastical Christianity, Friedrich Nietzsche, passionate antagonist and mocker of all Christendom — 'God is dead', Christianity is the 'only immortal stain of shame on humanity' — of course the personal relationship to Christianity of such a man must be a more than attractive complex of problems. A mere glance at the now rather comprehensive bibliography may assure us of this.

Nietzsche, however, has not been attractive mainly to anti-Christian investigators seeking an arsenal of arms for attacking Christendom. Though, of course, he has also been used for such a purpose, by enthusiastic adulators of Darwin in his lifetime, as well as by the Nazi ideologists of the Hitler period. But these 'Nietzschians' do not represent the main currents of interest in Nietzsche. His explosions are too violent, his characterizations have too little shading; those who want to expose the weakness of the church may find other and less problematical arsenals at hand.

For this reason, the subject has provoked no great number of Christian apologists to provide any convincing refutation of the criticism. Nietzsche's preoccupation with Christianity has become a captivating subject especially for those who see the riddle — a complex of contrarieties where Christian and anti-Christian elements seem sometimes to jostle each other, sometimes to entangle each other and to combine in rather surprising patterns, and sometimes to be absorbed by each other, to disappear inside each other — for those, briefly, who sense a hidden accusation of Western culture and Western Christianity, or indeed these very entities accusing themselves, *behind* the manifest accusations which, in his own phrase, the old 'artillerist' Nietzsche lets fly at his target.

Already in 1896 a treatise introduces Nietzsche as an 'Educator to Christianity', and four years later another asks, 'Nietzsche's mission, Christian or modernistic?' Several interpreters find symptoms of an approaching reconversion in the time immediately before Nietzsche's spiritual development was suddenly stopped by mental disease at the New Year 1888-89. In a study on Nietzsche dating from 1923 the Swedish philosopher *Alf Ahlberg* sums up many of the spiritual features which Nietzsche shares with Christianity, above all the emphasis on the importance and responsibility of the individual. 'Between the efforts of the Christian mystics to become like God, and the efforts of the superman to become God, the inherent difference is perhaps not essential.'

In recent years very characteristic and very different religious interpretations of Nietzsche have appeared. He has been hailed by theological liberalism as the rediscoverer of the Gospel and its liberator from all theological forgeries; after all doesn't he acclaim the 'historical' Jesus and abjure the whole ecclesiastical process of dogmatization? He has been saluted by Catholics as an impulse toward scholastic revival; after all doesn't he rehabilitate 'nature' against the whole Protestant discrimination? And he has been interpreted by the great existentialist thinker *Karl Jaspers* as at the same time a representative and a reformer of the Christian philosophical tradition, as an advocate for a Christianity drained of all mythological elements and restored to its essential glory as a 'naked challenge'.

Let this enumeration serve as a preliminary indication that Nietzsche's preoccupation with Christianity is less simple and unambiguous than a first glance might lead one to believe. Between his many unrestrained and furious attacks there is sometimes a little outburst of love to be detected, at least enough to indicate that the fury must result from an unfinished and unsettled dispute, a dispute that hurts precisely because it *is* unresolved.

I cannot, of course, give here any broad survey of Nietzsche's concern with Christianity, nor, in addition, of his interpreters' preoccupation with this preoccupation of his. Instead I shall try to isolate some single theme, in order to outline, if possible, the basic tendency of his religious development. A strictly chronological exposition, then, will not be the most useful one; we should rather try to grasp the motivation of his first open attack on Christianity and afterwards consider his motivation in the light both of the struggles of his youth, as far as these can be traced, and of the works of his maturity.

1.

It has become customary to divide Nietzsche's development into different stages. His biographers talk of his idealistic period, determined by Schopenhauer and Wagner, his positivistic period, dominated by the nineteenth-century veneration of Science, and, finally, his period of 'revaluation' *(Umwertung)* and his intensive efforts to make himself totally independent. This division would, no doubt, be of great importance if we wanted to examine his concept of science, or his criticism of his own age. But the situation is not quite the same when we turn to look at his religious conflict. As we shall soon see, the different 'periods' show that, for some time, he believed he had found his personal ideal realized in new environments, but this ideal itself turns out to have remained comparatively constant. This does not change; it only undergoes a process of differentiation and definition.

An objection immediately arises. Nietzsche did not launch any attack on Christianity until he did so in his work *Human—Much too Human (Menschliches, Allzumenschliches)*, that is, until his 'positivistic' period. Isn't this rather remarkable? Before that time he had in his first *Unseasonable Meditation (Unzeitgemässe Betrachtung)* punished D. F. Strauss, the celebrated radical theologian, hero of the so-called cultivated classes, who wanted, in the name of modern culture, to do away with the gospels as completely mythological products, and to canonize the vague, romantic religiosity of these same classes. In his attack on Strauss, Nietzsche betrays not the least tendency to sympathize with him and his rejection of historical Christianity. And in another of his early works, *The Birth of Tragedy from the Spirit of Music,* he has already introduced and put up against each other the two basic ideals of spiritual life, the 'Apollonian' and the 'Dionysiac', a distinction which was soon to become very important for his criticism of Christianity: Platonic 'Apollonism' and the Jewish cult of suffering and hatred together make Christianity, the typical religion of inferiors and slaves. Dionysus plunges himself into seething life, Apollo holds himself apart from it. But even in this work Christianity is left in silence, 'cautious and inimical silence' he himself calls it in his preface sixteen years later. Since Nietzsche does not attack Christianity in the works mentioned, even on occasions which would some years later have been more than sufficient to provoke such attacks, does not this argue a rather decisive change in his relation to Christianity during these years?

I am not convinced. *Human — Much too Human* does to some extent seek support in a positivistic theory of religion and morality: Religion is an attempt of prescientific man to secure control of the unknown forces of Nature. But it isn't at this point in the book that we find the real emotional core of Nietzsche's criticism of Christianity. This is evidently to be found in another idea: 'Christianity un-Greek — The Greeks did not consider the Homeric gods their masters, nor did they consider themselves their slaves. They found in them, let me say, the images of the most successful specimens of their own cast, ideals of what men can be, not of what men must be forever set apart from. Man has a distinguished concept of himself when he gives himself such gods, he chooses a relation to them almost like that of the lower nobleman to the higher ... Christianity, on the contrary, subjugated man and broke him totally to pieces and sank him down in deep mud ... There is only one thing it completely denies, *das Maass,* and therefore it is, in the deepest sense, barbarian, Asiatic, undistinguished, un-Greek.'

'Das Maass' — here we have found an expression of the thing we are searching for. The word must here be taken in the sixth of the ten senses given in Grimm's *Deutsches Wörterbuch*: '*der volle Gehalt des einem Zugemessenen*' ('The full contents of something rightfully attributed to someone'). The English equivalent would be 'measure', but I fear this word does not exactly fit. The point is clear, however: Christianity tries to withhold from man something which rightfully belongs to him, his mark of nobility, his kinship with the gods. From here we can discern a direct line leading to the statement in *Will to Power*: 'When the Greek body and the Greek soul were flourishing... that symbol, rich with secrets, of world-affirmation and illumination of existence higher than any which has until now been seen on earth, arose. Here is given a measure *(Maasstab)*, at which everything, that has grown since then, proves too short, too poor, too narrow... Dionysus is a *judge!*'

But already in his *Birth of Tragedy* Nietzsche has proclaimed himself as a disciple of Dionysus — why then does this Dionysus not appear as the judge of Christianity till nearly ten years after his own 'birth'? I think the answer is to be found in a single name: *Richard Wagner,* the great composer. In *The Birth of Tragedy* Wagner is hailed as the reborn Dionysus. His heroic music is going to redeem mankind, and the mystical union between man and existence will then be regenerated. But—alas!—in the meantime Wagner has capitulated and made himself a traitor to his own cause. His *Parsifal* droops down powerless before the cross of Christ — at this tree of shame Dionysus is annihilated, Apollo and all evil powers are triumphant again. Wagner 'is making love to obscurantist tendencies', Nietzsche states, for want of new ideas he is borrowing anything he can find, even 'Christian sentiments'.

In this situation it becomes clear to Nietzsche that he has misunderstood and overesteemed Richard Wagner. He had experienced Dionysus in the Wagnerian music, certainly, but this 'Wagner' was not really Wagner, it was himself. At that very moment, precisely what he took to be the treason of

Wagner, made the gulf between Dionysus and Christ acutely felt. From this deception on, his fight for Dionysus is at the same time a fight against Christ. But his basic ideal is by no means changed. Dionysus, the apotheosized and god-possessed man, is essentially the same, whether Nietzsche sees him incarnate in the *Meistersinger* or in the pathetic disciple of science, the 'free spirit'.

2.

Let us then see how the Dionysiac line, which links together the romantic and the positivistic periods of Nietzsche's authorship, may be traced back through the years of his youth.

The inward process of fermentation which led to his personal break with Christianity, is testified in a large number of notes and records from the age of seventeen to twenty-one. The years before this crisis seem to have been dominated by a personal piety in the orthodox Lutheran spirit. In some autobiographical retrospections the young Nietzsche takes particular pleasure in dwelling on God's paternal guidance and protection. And thanks to his rich musical and poetic disposition he met in the church chorale a particular stimulus toward religious commitment, which may be seen especially from his own attempts as a hymn writer and composer of church music, attempts which had been going on for several years.

No doubt, therefore, Karl Jaspers is wrong in maintaining that Nietzsche's Christianity already in his childhood consisted of a pure existential 'challenge', void of any dogmatic contents: 'Christianity, as contents of belief and dogma, is alien to him from the very beginning; his Christianity is nothing but a human truth dressed in symbols'. Jaspers founds his conclusion on two records from 1862. First, 'The basic doctrines of Christianity only express the main truths of the human heart ... Getting blessed by faith means nothing except the old truth that only the heart, not knowledge, can make a man happy. God having become man will only indicate that man should not seek his bliss in infinity, but establish his heaven on earth'.

And secondly, 'Decisive revolts are still approaching, when the multitude starts to conceive that Christianity is based entirely upon suppositions. The existence of God, immortality, authority of Holy Scriptures, inspirations etc. will always remain problems. I have tried to deny it all: Oh, razing is easy, but constructing!' Considered quite separately these records might perhaps be interpreted in the direction of the 'loss of all Christian contents', advocated by Karl Jaspers. The matter itself is, however, far more complicated than this, and in the records from the years of fermentation enough material can be found which does not fit into the theory.

Two years after the records underlined by Jaspers we find two conflicting testimonies, both related to Nietzsche's graduation and dismissal from the high school at Pforta. Here we see how he must have lived in a kind of tension between two incompatible concepts of God. In one of the records he resumes his thanks to all those whom he feels indebted to on looking backward from this milestone of his life. He starts by expressing his thanks to God, in warm wording he commemorates God's loving protection and concludes: 'Oh, might He also henceforth protect me, my faithful God!' But an entirely different tune echoes through his famous poem, dedicated to an unknown God:

> Ich will dich kennen, Unbekannter,
> Du tief in meine Seele Greifender,
> Mein Leben wie ein Strohm durchschweifender
> Du Unfassbarer, mir Verwandter!
> Ich will dich kennen, selbst dir dienen.

A translation of this expressive stanza can hardly be given without losing a good deal of its meaning. May I therefore suggest a version in, comparatively, plain prose: 'I want to know Thee, Unknown Being, Thou who art grasping deep into my soul, sweeping through my life like a stream, Inconceivable Being and yet my kinsman. I want to know Thee and *myself* to serve Thee.' Two concepts here oppose one another: the God of Christianity, the loving father sheltering and protecting the children of mankind, and the God Unknown, the mystical relative of man, sweeping through the heroic soul, whom the soul tries to grasp in an emphatic, 'I want to know Thee . . .'

Space does not allow a broad exposition of the interesting records left from the years 1861-65. Let me confine myself to a few examples. From 1862 we know, besides the two fragments quoted by Karl Jaspers, a hymn in perfectly traditional style, but indisputably expressive of personal experience: 'Thou hast me called: my Lord I'm coming'. From 1863 we know a remarkable poem, 'In front of the Crucifix': a drunken fellow fiercely attacks a crucifix and destroys it. The poem is not easy to interpret, but seems to reveal that Nietzsche's own, very intense, preoccupation with the scene of the crucifixion contains a complex of conflicting feelings. As late as during the Easter holidays of 1864 the poem 'Gethsemane and Golgotha', which he has written down in no less than three different versions, betrays thoroughgoing meditations on the drama of the passion. This time too, it is the style as well as the theology of Lutheran orthodoxy that prevails:

> O Stätten heiligster Vergangenheit,
> Gethsemane und Golgatha, ihr tönet
> Die frohste Botschaft durch die Ewigkeit:
> Ihr kündet, dass der Mensch mit Gott versöhnet,
> Versöhnet durch das Herz, das hier gerungen,
> Das dort verblutet und den Tod bezwungen.

> Oh, places of the holy history,
> Gethsemane and Golgotha, you're sounding
> The happiest message through Eternity,
> That man with God is reconciled. Abounding
> Is grace thanks to the heart that here contending
> Has shed its blood and brought on Death its ending.

I ask you to bear in mind that this verse was written two years after the records invoked by Karl Jaspers, and just a few months before the graduation and the conception of the poem to the unknown God. How should this, as it were, consistent inconsistency be interpreted? Can Nietzsche at the same time have found spiritual nourishment in both traditional ecclesiastical piety and in a somewhat pantheistic mysticism completely void of 'Christian contents'? His letters and records betray no consciousness of being torn between two religious concepts. Perhaps the apparent contradictions may be resolved by some deeper, uniting motive?

Let us take a new look at the two fragments from 1862: The first of them, reducing Christianity to 'main truths of the human heart', ends by pointing at the incarnation, which it conceives as a supposition in the 'glowing juvenile soul of mankind' of the divine humanity which will exist when a fully mature mankind one day discovers in itself 'the origin, the center and the aim of religion'. In other words, what the record looks forward to is a future deification of the human race. The other record, bearing the heading 'Fate and History', reflects doubt, doubt above all in the possibility of finding another basis for those who reject Christianity, because they are scared by its uncertainty. How can we reach any assurance at all, chained as we are to the process of history without being able to interpret it? But eventually, at the end of Nietzsche's meditation one possibility seems to dawn on the horizon: '... as soon as it would be possible, by means of a strong will, to overthrow the whole past of this world, then we should at once have been promoted to the rank of independent gods, and world history would then have become to us nothing more than a dreamlike absence from ourselves. The curtain must fall, and man find himself again, like a child playing with globes, like a child who wakes up at dawn, and laughing, sweeps the dreadful dreams from its brow'.

Is there any connection between this mythological child playing with globes, and the child of Biblical terminology talking to its heavenly father? More exactly, can the hymn writer Nietzsche, with his intense engagement in what may technically be called the mythos of Christianity, the religious psychologist Nietzsche, with his disposition for picking historical revelation to pieces, and the mythologist Nietzsche, with his apparent roots in the Greek-Roman world of tales and legends — be understood as representatives of some common effort? I think they can. Even in the spring of 1866, that is, at the time when

106

his admiration for *Schopenhauer* was at its strongest, Nietzsche, writing in a letter in which he denounces Christianity in the sense of 'belief in an historical fact', proclaims his adherence to the Christian doctrine of a universal 'need of redemption'. Redemption — redemption in the sense of a heroic drama, through which man is breaking through his immediate limitations and grasping an absolute aim, an unconditioned fullness of humanity — which includes a fullness of divinity — *there* is the theme which may be said to bear his multitude of seemingly competing religious endeavors.

Space prevents me from pointing out in detail the influence of *Goethe, Hölderlin, Byron* and others, which, together with an even more comprehensive acquaintance with classical Antiquity, influenced his personal development during these years. Exactly that which we have seen him present later on as 'Greek' religiosity, is already taking shape in his mind. This is what he is groping for, this is what he suspects an echo of, now in historical Christianity, now in a reinterpretation of it according to rationalistic and/or romantic paradigms. As the discrepancy between historical Christianity and his own ideal of redemption gradually comes to his consciousness, the need of a new redeemer grows urgent.

The soil was now prepared for the meeting with Schopenhauer in the autumn of 1865. There are some quite touching testimonies of the youthful cult of the great prophet of philosophical pessimism in the little circle of student converts in Leipzig who, persuaded by the word of Nietzsche, came to faith. To Nietzsche Schopenhauer became for a while the true and only revelation. Here he found human Will revealed as the basic mystery of existence — here he got decisive assistance in separating his myth of redemption from the belief in an historical revelation. But the spell soon started to dwindle: Schopenhauer not only reveals the power of human will, he also denounces it; his denial of life is another attempt to lay the Greek in chains. We have already seen how, in the same way, the next prophet of Dionysus, Wagner, became a deception.

All the time the guiding question seems to have been the one he puts to *D. F. Strauss,* and by means of which he defeats the 'dogmaless' religion of that writer: 'How does the man of the new faith imagine his heaven? . . . How far does the courage reach, which that new faith is granting him?' In other words, what kind of a redemption does he promise? Strauss is rejected because his heaven consists in nothing more than an abandonment of anything exceeding average bourgeois boredom. Thus the 'new faith' is rejected on exactly the same premisses as is, later on, the old one: it is 'undistinguished, un-Greek'; it denies human kinship with the gods. Dionysus, the judge, is judging Strauss as he is going to judge Schopenhauer, as he is going to judge Wagner, as he has, in Nietzsche's heart, already judged historical Christianity. That much is presented in *Human — Much too Human*. In *Beyond Good and Evil* the positivists, in their turn, are included: 'They belong, to put it shortly and roughly, among the levellers, these titular "free spirits".'

Christianity, romanticism, positivism, the same tribunal judges each of them in their turn, pronouncing every time the same verdict, 'Decadent!' What, according to Nietzsche, is decadence? It is a fading of the very will to life and, therefore, a perversion of Nature itself. It is a denial of the Greek ideal of man, or perhaps, rather, of the man of the Greek ideal. Again and again Nietzsche believes himself to have found what he is seeking, again and again he has to declare himself disappointed.

### 3.

Is his criticism of Christianity, then, no more than a link in a long and consistent chain of criticisms: the church disappoints, Schopenhauer disappoints, Wagner disappoints, Comte disappoints, so at last he stands there completely desolate? No, such an explanation would not do justice to the inexhaustible occupation with Christianity that is apparent from his works. None of his other ex-gods engaged him to the same extent as did the God of Christianity.

His indefatigable circling around Christianity must have

been to some extent determined also by the portrait of history which was gradually taking shape before his eyes. Christianity thus became responsible for modern civilization in its entire decadence, the God of Christianity becoming the real traitor, hidden also in Nietzsche's many other deceitful gods. It was He who had created democracy, levelling, compassion — everything in modern culture which was unhealthy, un-Greek and life-hampering. The debilitation of man, for which Christianity and Christianity alone was responsible, was everywhere prevalent in modern culture, in its rationalistic as well as in its religious forms.

This evaluation of the influence of Christianity in his own time, is closely connected with his conception of its origin. His occupation with that issue may be studied, above all, in *Anti-Christ* and *The Will to Power*. In these works Nietzsche pursues and develops a line from *The Birth of Tragedy*: Christianity is 'Platonism for the people', a piece of Jewish ideology adapting everything in Antiquity which is un-Dionysiac and un-Homeric, thus making itself victorious by appealing to the instinct of the plebeians. With some reference to the criticism of the gospels in nineteenth-century theology, which Nietzsche must have known, partly from his own studies, partly through his good friend, the rather radical theologian *Franz Overbeck*, Nietzsche renews the popular thesis of a gulf between Jesus and successive ecclesiastical developments. He does not hesitate to judge the whole New Testament as forgery, and thus to discharge Jesus of Nazareth from every responsibility for the Christian religion.

'As a matter of fact there has only existed one Christian, and he died on the cross.' '"Christianity" is something basically different from the actions and the purposes of its founder.' Nietzsche is not content, as were his predecessors *Renan* and *Strauss*, to put Jesus in opposition to the ecclesiastical process of dogmatization; above all, he puts him in opposition to the nineteenth-century bourgeoisie and its ideals. His Jesus is a political anarchist who disavows civil society with all its codes and regulations. A writer of whom this idea may readily remind us is *Leo Tolstoy*. It has been a point of discussion whether

Nietzsche's *Anti-Christ* should be taken as dependent upon Tolstoy's *In what consists my belief?* It seems to me that the 'proofs' which have been offered for and against such a dependency are inconclusive. In any case one decisive difference remains between the two: Even if Nietzsche gives Jesus an advantage over the church, the advantage is not such as might cause Nietzsche to be greatly enthusiastic. The honest Nazarene, preaching denial of this world as the only way to happiness and inward strength, might perhaps have touched him during his Schopenhauerian period — but now he has done with him, even before he has discovered him. This figure is an accidental product of his occupation with the origin of Christianity, of his searching for the disappeared Dionysus. But it is itself no incarnation of Dionysus; rather, a melancholic reflection of something which had once to him appeared as an incarnation, one of the many bubbles which burst, Schopenhauer.

Entirely different are his feelings toward the Christ of the Church. 'The Crucified' is by and by becoming a pure type, the Anti-Dionysus, the very focus of the mythology of decadence, the soul of a cult where everything mean and petty and false is triumphant, and therefore, the object of the most fervent hatred for the Dionysiac man. 'Dionysus against the crucified, there you have the opposition . . . Tragic man accepts even the bitterest suffering; he is strong, full, divine enough for that. Christian man denies even the happiest fate on earth; he is weak, poor, disinherited enough to feel life a suffering in whatever form. The God on the cross is a curse thrown upon life — an advice to redeem oneself from him. Dionysus, cut in pieces, is a promise of life: life will ever be renascent and overcome destruction . . . Have you understood me? Dionysus against the Crucified . . .'

'God is dead' — what is the meaning of this frequently repeated maxim? Two things seem immediately evident. The statement is not to be considered as a metaphysical one, 'dead' is not an exact equivalent for 'non-existent'. Nor is it a simple piece of cultural analysis: God is no living reality in modern culture. If we gather together the many different contexts in which the statement occurs, the following will be clear.

Nietzsche's judgment is meant as a judgment upon the Christian tradition, not only this tradition in its possible self-apostasy, but exactly in its deepest intentionality. The fellowship with God, preached by this tradition — and including all its modern degenerate forms — is a mere fiction, and a new era approaching will make this apparent and thus overthrow every foundation of Western culture. Only in Dionysiac mysticism is God alive, that is, God called to life by Superman. 'God is dead, and it is high time that Superman were living', Zarathustra proclaims. 'Once people said God when they surveyed distant oceans; but now I have taught you to say Superman. God is a measure of courage; but I don't want your masses of courage to reach further than your creative will. — Are you able to create a god? — Then be silent of all gods! But surely you can create the superman.' The consistency between this denial of God in *Thus spoke Zarathustra* and the praise of the Greek gods in *Human—Much too Human* is apparent. The question of God's existence does not occupy his interest at all. Belief itself in a God involves for Nietzsche the dethroning of that very God one pretends to believe in. The point is to make divinity a reality here and now. Only incarnate in the heroic fullness of will, in Superman, does the deity become real to his imagination. What is truly significant is, 'The supreme richness of life, present in the Dionysiac god-and-man'.

Then, of course, the finishing touches are put to the scheme by the doctrine of 'The eternal return of identities'. Here his *Lust* is finding its 'deep, deep Eternity'. In his concept of repetition the religious idea of history as a meaningful entity — and the existence of the single human as part, or in any case a potential part, of this all-comprehensive meaning — is regained. But it is no longer a celestial Lord who is giving an aim to history and leading the current of events toward it; it is the apotheosized human will. The Dionysiac motif develops into a global view of the phenomena; under the leadership of the legendary hero Zarathustra the Homeric world arises anew. The life-affirming preaching of Zarathustra 'is the idea of Dionysus once more'. On this background it can scarcely be right to assume, as does the German scholar *Grützmacher*, that

Nietzsche started to dress his Zarathustra in religious garments just for pedagogical reasons, and that, trapped in the consequences of some general law, he became the slave of his own symbolic language, so that eventually the symbols turned into something more than symbols. On the contrary, it is natural to imagine the whole further progress of events as a consistent development — intentionally I don't say fulfillment — of the youth prayer, 'I want to know Thee, unknown Being.'

Perhaps the development may be traced even further back. From the age of ten there is extant a little 'Comedy' entitled 'The Tempted Man', intended to be played by himself and a few friends. The subject is chosen from Antiquity. The noble Sirenius is helping Jupiter, the latter disguised and seemingly badly off. As a reward he is being promoted to the pantheon of the gods. Nymphs are sent to summon him into the waves of the sea. The parents are standing on the beach mourning their lost son. Then, suddenly, Sirenius appears before them. 'Oh, dear son, why did you yield to enticement?' the mother asks. 'Oh, don't you worry! Oh, how happy I am! A demigod I am now.'

4.

In his criticism of Christianity Nietzsche acts as the main inheritor of a theme which, in different forms, may be said to have dominated the whole of German Idealism — Faust, or man seeking deification. Thus he is a descendant of Christian mysticism, as well as an echoer of the *eritis sicut dii* that constitutes the basic theme of the Biblical report of the fall. The Christian answer to this has been given its classical form by the famous Danish theologian and poet *Grundtvig* in his poem *De Levendes Land*. Here the poet bids farewell to the myth of Romanticism, 'the deceitful dream / of island eternal in temporal stream'; 'the demigod life', as he also calls it.

But, on the other hand, let us note the commentary on Nietzsche by the outstanding German philosopher *Georg Simmel*: ' "There cannot exist any God", he said, "for if he had existed, how could I have stood not to be God myself?" But however fantastic and excessive this may sound, he is in this regard only giving expression to the highest feeling of personalism, which in other expressions is not unfamiliar even to Christian currents of inwardness. In Christianity there is, besides all the experience of difference and debasement with respect to God, alway the ideal of a life of becoming "like" him'.

Let this be admitted. Let us even add that Nietzsche's passionate demand for integrity and his emphasis on the infinite importance of individual man, are consistent with Christian concepts. It must, however, be stressed that his basic ideal of life, apart from all verbal exaggerations, is anti-Christian. He denies the equality in guilt and the equality in value of all men. And he denies the atonement between God and man achieved by the divine Mediator. 'The Crucified' is, as he clearly realized, the absolute contrary of Dionysus and thus of 'that paramount joy, where man experiences himself, and himself entirely, as a deified form and self-justification of Nature'.

And yet, why does Nietzsche, after his great mental collapse, sign his letters sometimes 'Dionysus', sometimes 'the Crucified'? The coherent line we have pointed out, the development of the 'Greek' conception of life, does not reveal the whole truth about Nietzsche and Christianity. The psychological play in its complex diversity is left concealed. But probably we have touched on the idea which, surely more than any other, connected his life with his thought, and vice versa: Dionysus — the redeemer of man. Christ did not fill the part, nor Schopenhauer, nor Wagner, nor any of the positivists. Nietzsche himself did, but — not till the very moment when he exclaimed, 'The world is transfigured and all heavens are rejoicing.' The world transfigured — yes, indeed — in the flash which followed the short circuit and signalized the entry of his soul into that inescapable darkness which was to comprise the rest of his days.

# VII

## The Dilemma of Contemporary Theology

As a pupil at elementary school some twenty years ago, I used to wonder why the history text-book ended with the year 1905 (a rather decisive date in the history of my country). One of my fellow-pupils one day asked the teacher why, and I still remember his answer. 'You cannot write history', he said, 'till all those who made it are dead — or else there would be a terrible commotion. Only when a man is resting peacefully in his grave may you say of him whatever you like without causing any trouble.'

This is, indeed, a simplification, but I should think rather an impressive one. When you talk to people about problems sufficiently remote, in time or in space, problems with which they are not personally concerned, you may always feel safe. As will be seen, I have chosen most of the items for my essays in this collection from safely distant fields. None of my readers is directly involved in the subjects in such a way that my statements could possibly be felt as judgments upon his personal theological endeavors.

The present item will make a fairly definite exception. When I speak of 'contemporary theology', everyone who is involved in some kind of theological activity is immediately concerned. In fact I do exactly what my old teacher taught me not to do and behave like an unwise historian. *Si tacuisses philosophus permansisses,* goes an old saying; 'If you had kept your mouth shut, you would have kept your reputation as a philosopher'. However, I think it would be wrong of me to confine my

114

comments to distant fields just in order to preserve a reputation — either as a philosopher, as an historian, or as a theologian. It is right that I should be expected to point out the principal needs of our present theological thinking, and to establish the link between the various more or less, geographically or historically remote fields and our own immediate concerns.

## 1.

When speaking of 'contemporary' theology, or perhaps even more of 'modern' theology, many of us immediately feel a little uneasy; isn't theology a thing which ought not to change with the changing times? God is the same, man is essentially the same, the Devil is the same — how can man's understanding of his connections with the one or the other be shifting, supposing that the understanding in itself be true?

Shouldn't our topic then be formulated 'The Dilemma of Theology', *not* 'The Dilemma of *Contemporary* Theology'? No doubt this alternative formulation would have provided an equally interesting and important theme — but to a large extent a different one. 'There are many roads leading to Rome', says an old proverb. That doesn't indicate that there are many Romes, but just that there are travellers starting from different places and moving in different directions. Thus, 'going to Rome' and 'walking from Ostia to Rome' would make two different themes for a lecture. So also in their understanding of our Christian faith, different times and different cultures start with different qualifications. 'We don't reflect ourselves into Christianity, but we reflect ourselves out of non-Christian conditions and in becoming more and more simple, we enter into Christianity', says Kierkegaard in his *Concluding Unscientific Postscript.*

These non-Christian conditions, which our theological reflections have to discover and to lead away from, have to be recognized in their different disguises at different times. All human beings in all historical situations are the same sinners needing the same salvation, but their sameness has to be discovered through thick layers of historical variety. That is the reason why Christian preaching and Christian thinking cannot merely confine themselves to the repeating of canonized words. Our task is to bring a never-changing message through ever-changing symbols and notions. As soon as this task is set in a single historical situation, the problem of a 'contemporary' theology will arise: how can *our* time be confronted with the Gospel; how can the Church of *today* avoid presenting a false scandal by a cult of antiquated words and forms; how can it avoid abandoning the true scandal in succumbing to man-pleasing fashions? — How is theology today facing these questions; along which lines is it seeking its answers; to what extent are satisfactory answers really being found?

Though the contents of our faith are not subject to historical alterations, the framework of human comprehension is. Let us just glance at church history to see how this fact has been realized and interpreted. Already to the Greek fathers, and especially perhaps to the Alexandrian school, the need to get in contact with contemporary thought appeared urgent. The Alexandrians interpreted and translated the Gospel from the Hebrew into the Hellenistic cultural sphere. Their endeavor was given a religious motivation through the doctrine of the λόγος σπερματικός: the Word a scattered seed, sown by God in the hearts even of noble pagan thinkers. The Stoic and Platonic thinkers had not been able to locate the source of the light, but definitely they had felt its beams, and definitely their ideas were instruments appropriate for the propagation of the Gospel.

Today it is easy to see how these venerable fathers overstrained themselves. Look, for example, at the tragic career of the great *Origen*: in his work it is more than obvious that the historic revelation has to a large extent been devoured by that disastrous idea of a substantial revelation outside Scripture. Here we have a doctrine of man, and a belief in man, which is fairly incompatible with the Biblical representation of sin and grace. But on the other hand we have to admit that our Creeds also, the Nicene as well as the Athanasian, to a large extent speak the language of the Hellenistic world — not in order to accommodate Christian belief whithin Hellenistic religion, but in order to ward off any such accommodating. The Church here spoke the language of its secular neighborhood, not to make the challenge harmless, but to make it heard.

During the Middle Ages *the Roman idea of revelation* becomes more and more clear and distinct. Revelation is not a thing that has happened, but a thing that is happening. Revelation is a continuous process in the church. In principle the whole truth has been planted in the world through the institution of the Catholic church. But different germs of the plant have been destined to sprout in the course of history. To realise this is to realise also that the doctrine of the church can never be revised; its only mode of change is growth. New statements and new conceptions may be added, but they can never contradict the previous ones. Theology, however, is subject to change in a somewhat wider sense. Roman theologians are allowed to maintain their personal opinions in so far as these opinions are not contrary to the official doctrines of the church. This means that in questions which have not been definitely decided by the church Roman theologians may hold different viewpoints. Thus also within the Roman church a theological discussion is made possible, although within rather definite limits. Moreover, the church can even be said to encourage attempts to interpret Christianity in new terms. Through this relative theological freedom a constant process of spiritual segregation and clarification is taking place, which by-and-by renders it possible for the Pope to bring new areas under the authority of official ecclesiastical dogma. A question which is under discussion today may be under the bond of authority a hundred years hereafter.

Inside this well-closed system a real basic dilemma can never arise. The dilemma will always be a dilemma outside it, of the form, Does this-and-this idea which the church commands me to believe, fit in with facts which I really know and which I cannot possibly look away from? But the system itself is coherent and clear and provokes no real objections from within. In the practical life of the church, however, the conflict between, say, Dominican orthodoxy and Jesuit accommodationalism has never been definitely settled. Even in our day Jesuit fathers can be reproached by the Holy Seat for their tendency to stretch

dogmatic sentences to bring them closer to the thought of outside groups. Even if the limits of orthodoxy are stated quite
clearly in the official decisions of the church, every statement
in this world is subject to interpretations. Therefore it may now
and then be necessary for the Pope to emphasize that such-and-
such an interpretation (set forth by Mr. So-and-so), is not per-
mitted. Usually, Mr. So-and-so will immediately submit to the
decision. So much for the Roman position.

What then about the Reformation? *Martin Luther's* point
was not to reform theology in the sense of bringing it into
closer contact with a new age. On the contrary, one may say, his
concern was to reorientate its affiliation backward, to re-estab-
lish contact with its original source. As most of my readers will
probably know, his first polemical step against the Roman
church was not taken in pinning the ninety-five Theses against
the misuse of indulgence to the door of the royal chapel in Wittenberg, but in issuing his far sharper theses against Aristotelian
theology a month or two earlier. As the indulgence business
barred the way to justification by faith to the ordinary man
and woman, Aristotelian philosophy barred the way to the
understanding of justification to the theologian. Instead of submitting humbly to the Word of God contained in Holy Scriptures, the theologians founding their systems on Aristotelian
philosophy paid homage to human wisdom and pride. They
exalted themselves and promoted themselves to judges in their
own case instead of accepting the judgment of the living God.

Does this criticism imply that Luther himself wanted to confine theology to a mere reproduction of Biblical notions and
formulations? His rather free translation of the Scriptures, together with the frank use of his mother tongue in his sermons
and lectures, will lead us to a somewhat different conclusion. As
also expressed in the famous preface to his German New Testament translation, the apostolic word is the word 'driving Christ',
or rather, we should nowadays say, 'emphasizing Christ'. The
message of sin and grace is a message beyond anything we could
find out and learn by ourselves. This message, which no philosophy can help us to attain, must be told us by God Himself.

118

That is why Holy Writ must be the only source of true theology. But Luther is fully aware of the distance between Jerusalem and Wittenberg, and for good reasons he becomes the great translator. The translation itself, however, by no means occurs to him as a separate theological problem. He has made his great discovery in Scripture, and he never ceases to point out to us what he has discovered. But details in Scripture which seem to contradict his discovery are not taken too seriously, nor are Copernicus and the rising scientific endeavors of his time — these are considered just fruits of human pride.

The problem of theological adjustment to his own time did not appear to Luther in the same way as it has appeared to theology throughout almost its entire history. Although not so fanatical as to exclude all the previous life of the church, or to know no other ambassadors of true Christianity than 'the Bible and I' — he had to say farewell to the ecclesiastical camp and seek his own way. This meant freedom from tradition in a much wider sense than will ever be possible in normal situations of church life, even within the most spiritually spiritual Assembly-of-God congregation. Thanks to his philological genius, he found in his German *Sprache* an instrument with new possibilities for expressing the message. A new theology preached in a new language to a church in vivid renewal involves an adjustment to its environment without expressly searching for it.

This is also the reason why a Lutheran church — a church sharing Luther's discovery of the center of Scripture as well as of the central position of Scripture in a sound theology — in the course of her history will have to face the adjustment problem in a way in which Luther was never forced to face it. We are living in something which he was not living in — a Lutheran tradition. What to Luther was a vision, is to us (I hope) the same, but it is also (I know) something more, and, in a sense, something widely different. We are not able to speak the language of our time to the same extent as Luther was able to speak the language of his, just because he spoke that language so extremely well. We are forced, consciously or unconsciously, to mimic him. We are not imitating Luther only, of course, but

119

some hundred other voices of distinguished fathers, who have together contributed to what may be called the general voice of our church. But we cannot be free to the same extent as was Martin Luther, and we should not even try to be.

There are two temptations to theology: the temptation of *mimicking* the fathers and the temptation of *ignoring* them; both are detrimental to the true virtue of *listening*. The first of them has been the traditional sin of orthodoxy, the second the sin of heterodoxy. But both these 'sinners' are right in the following observations: the church has a far wider experience and understanding of Christian truth than I (orthodoxy); the church can neither think nor believe for me (heterodoxy).

As you will have noticed I am all the time concerned with our actual theme, 'contemporary' theology. So don't worry if the formal approach will still take its time. I just need to gather the courage necessary to defy my old teacher's warning. Before arriving at the year 1960 it is necessary to say more about the roles played by orthodoxy and heterodoxy in the history of Protestantism. The function of one has been to underline the important fact that the Gospel is a given entity, a revelation which cannot be affected or altered by any human endeavor. The function of the other has been to underline the not unimportant fact that our faith is expressing itself in terms that are always subject to the conditions of changing historical life. Unhappily they have both shown tendencies to surpass the limits of these admittedly legitimate vocations.

I shall refrain from discussing here the classical monument of orthodox derailment, the doctrine of verbal inspiration in its seventeenth-century form. Let me just mention in passing the two facts, that this doctrine constituted a bar to historical as well as to scientific research, and that it tended to reduce theology into a debate about right words and to the building up of a system of holy terms. In the hymns and sermons of the seventeenth century, however, Luther's evangelical vision is still strongly alive. The vision can here and there also be discerned behind the theological constructions. But the tendency to found the belief in Christ on the belief in the Book was in itself contrary to Luther's principle, 'What is driving

120

Christ?' And, of course, if our belief in Christ is resting upon our belief in the Bible, then the whole orthodox theory with its inspired words, commas and periods becomes necessary. For the very foundation of our faith must be perfectly stable and sure. And then, consequently, we dare not step outside the divine vocabulary in our theological interpretations.

The theology of the *Enlightenment* during the latter half of the eighteenth and first quarter of the nineteenth centuries in many ways appears as the absolute anti-orthodoxy. Of particular interest in our study is the Enlightenment concept of perfectibility. The Christian religion is conceived as perfectible, that is to say, as coinciding with perfect religion somewhere in the future. History is a mighty process of development in which ideas find more and more adequate expression. The direction is forward, forward, constantly forward. Christ and the Apostles had to face a primitive epoch with rude and superstitious notions, and in order to give their contemporaries as much true religion as possible, they had to condescend to the spiritual level of their listeners. That is the reason why they had to arrange all those miracles, which, according to rationalistic theology, were merely natural events arranged with a certain amount of dexterity. Christ accommodated his teaching to the stupidity of his time, and so must we accommodate our teaching to that of ours — but to a considerably diminished and constantly decreasing stupidity as we look forward to the blessed day when the Church can tell things just as they are and become understood by a perfect mankind. Things as they are — the meaning of this was nothing but the traditional trinity of deism: 'God, virtue and immortality'.

As accommodation meant to orthodoxy a threat to true Christianity (in the sense of *Biblical* Christianity), to rationalism it also meant a threat to true Christianity (but in the sense of *future* Christianity). Also, to rationalism it became a concern not to go further in accommodation than was necessary for pedagogical reasons. But what rationalism fears getting distracted by is *primitive* man, the man who in his ignorance and indolence fears historical progress. What orthodoxy fears is falling prey to *natural* man, the man who in his self-complacency is opposing the kingdom of God. Here orthodoxy is obviously in an absolute right, and the rationalistic outlook only in a relative right. And orthodoxy will retain its right as long as it is able to withstand the temptation to identify natural man and regenerate man with men of particular different cultural spheres. Can anything more self-contradictory be imagined than a theology representing the seventeenth century in the twentieth, under the pretext of representing eternity in time? The limited right of rationalism was this: the Church should never be so attached to particular historical circumstances that it loses its freedom to meet and to deal with new historical circumstances. Its definite mistake was to equate new circumstances with better circumstances, and, consequently, to conceive history as an unbroken process of advance toward the happy end of perfect rationality.

After the collapse of eighteenth-century rationalism, we got *nineteenth-century liberal theology*. In one sense liberal theology carried forward the inheritance of the preceding age. The search for an appeasement between church and modern culture, for a peaceful co-existence between belief and science, ultimately led this movement to give away any element of the faith that did not fit into the 'modern' view of life. But the very essence of religion according to liberalism may also, in one way, be characterized as the absolute contrary of the rationalistic concept. Rationalism sought the essence of religion in a rational idea apt to serve as a moral motivation: its outlook is primarily intellectualistic and moralistic. And the basic principle is, or rather pretends to be, purely logical. The basic principle of liberal theology is, on the other hand, definitely psychological, its outlook mystical and emotional, its formula aptly expressed by *Wilhelm Hermann,* who found in Christianity a participation in 'the inner life of Jesus'. Christ is not considered the incarnate and resurrected Son of God in the orthodox and Biblical sense, nor a wise teacher and moral champion in the rationalistic sense; he is simply the explorer of a new and intimate way of human fellowship with God. In this respect he may even be invoked as divine, and where this fellowship is transplanted into pious hearts he may be said to be alive

122

and exercising his kingdom even after his death. Religion is, according to *Schleiermacher*, the father of this tradition, 'neither an understanding nor a practice, but a kind of immediate self-consciousness', 'a feeling of unconditioned dependence'. On this background, all the Biblical miracles are done away with, and only a spiritual miracle remains — the pious mind, propagating itself from individual to individual through the devout portrayal of the unique Christ.

In a way, this is a more religious understanding of religion than were the old rationalistic theories, but hardly a more congenial understanding of Christianity. The decisive point from a Biblical point of view is this: in liberal theology the trust of man is in a fatal way placed in himself. He is invited to put his confidence in religious life, not to put his religious life in confidence. His personal religious experience is the basis of everything; this experience has been made possible by Christ, who was the first man to make it, but as soon as it is mine, it is all mine. The undisturbed feeling of harmony with God is a propriety essential to the believing heart. My peace is resting, so to speak, in itself. In times of crisis and affliction, the thing needed is a deeper feeling of this divine life of mine. Perhaps some of my readers will recognize that they have met this kind of piety in circles by no means connected with liberal theology. In fact, liberal theology is only the consequent revelation of a piety with old roots in Western life, but one which has particularly been developed in the post-pietistic era, often under a thick cover of seeming Biblicism.

What this kind of piety can give no answer to is the urgent question of the sinner who has discovered the futility of his own efforts. When my own religious life appears to me as an obscure mixture of different motives — many of them shamefully egocentric — I can find no comfort whatsoever in possessed piety. I can only place my hope in someone outside me, someone different from me, someone offering to put himself in my place and me in his. I need Christ the Redeemer, not Christ the paradigm of perfect inward life. This sentimental business of inwardness becomes to me a kind of child's chatter, a concept that envisages neither sinful man nor righteous God. I refute it with the words of Anselm of Canterbury: 'You have never considered the oppression of sin.'

At the beginning of our own century we may point out a manifest alliance between the liberal belief in inwardness and the rationalistic doctrine of progress. Among the offspring of this alliance we find, for example, the theology of the social gospel, equating the growth of the pious mind in history with the progress of social development. Here the mystical inwardness of liberal theology has been changed into political outwardness, but the optimistic belief in piety is left unchanged, even if the kind of bliss to be obtained by piety has undergone transsubstantiation.

Just as the first big attack on orthodox Christianity, that of rationalism, was defeated by Romanticism with its deeper understanding of psychological life, so the second attack, that of liberal theology, was defeated by the first world war, which brought about a new discovery of human weakness and inflicted upon optimism its lethal wound. Rationalism had ignored feeling — that caused her ruin. Liberalism had ignored sin — that caused hers. The experience of the great war showed that the world is not marching incessantly forward and forward. Sometimes it is slipping backward, sometimes mankind is overwhelmed by demonic forces; sometimes it is precipitating itself into catastrophe. Who then can foresee the ultimate end?

This led, in the course of a few years, to an entire revolution in continental European theology, a revolution which has, as far as I can see, during the past generation transferred itself to the English-speaking world. To a certain extent this revolution has meant a general return to the orthodox view of man and of God. 'God is in heaven and you on earth', proclaimed the great theological champion of the era, *Karl Barth*. The proclamation is an echo of Soeren Kierkegaard: 'God is in heaven, I am on earth; therefore we cannot easily speak with each other.'

As Barthianism meant the victory of a new era within the particular field of theology, existentialism meant the same turning point within the general stream of thought. Positivism, the philosophical fashion of the previous generation, had tried to make a kind of science out of the belief in progress, and had found the essential mark of progress in its own unshakeable belief in science. Existentialism, in its great variety of shapes and schools, displays a general trend of distress and despair. Man has become aware of his absolute poverty. His belief in reason, in science, in humanity, are mere attempts to escape. Man's existence in this world is, in the words of *Martin Heidegger*, the father of existentialism, a '*Sein zum Tode*'. It is rather difficult to translate this term into English, but let me suggest the wording, 'a being tending toward Death'. Death in this connection appears mainly as an expression of total nonpossession. Man's conquest of the entire world is a mere illusion, because he is going to give his life away, which involves the total loss of all his conquest. Therefore a true human existence can be based upon nothing of what we seem to possess: wealth, science, morality, piety. All this is marked for death, all this is nothingness. True existence lies in the momentary choice of a personal self. I accept my absolute poverty, my death, my complete uncertainty as to the future — and choose to act without guarantees, only at my own risk. Thus existentialism must conclude in one of two opposite attitudes, a humble surrender to God's mercy, as with the French philosophers Mounier and Marcel, or in a titanic defiance of a merciless fate, as with Heidegger and Sartre.

The affinity that existentialist philosophy has with Barthian theology is not difficult to discern. Now, it is always a little difficult to talk of Barthianism, because Barth himself has undergone a never-ceasing process of development. The classical monuments of his period of rebellion are, above all, the second edition of his commentary on the letter to the Romans, and his *Christian Dogmatics*. The great *Ecclesiastical Dogmatics* from his later period involves, in many respects, a modification of his viewpoints and an approximation to traditional Calvinism. In talking of Barthianism we usually mean the Barth of the late twenties and early thirties, and the group behind the periodical, *Zwischen den Zeiten* (Between the Eras).

This Barthianism intends to be an exclusive 'theology of the Word of God'. Any revelation outside Christ and any belief in human religious qualities is abjured. Christianity is nothing but eschatology. Eschatology, however, does not imply events going to take place in history, but events beyond history. Belief in the Kingdom of God consequently means a total independence of anything that belongs to this world. History is placed under a complete judgment of God, and what the Gospel presents to us is the confidence in a mercy which no worldly appearance can reflect. In this world the Grace was, is and forever remains hidden, uncertain and improbable — it exists nowhere, except in the Word preached.

This Word is to be found in the Bible only, but it is not identical with the book. Barth's understanding of the word is markedly Christo-centric; to him even the creation becomes meaningful only through the belief in Christ. The word is the word only in the momentary meeting between the Kingdom promised and the servant submitting, submitting to a hope which is the unconditioned condemnation of all hopes we try to create ourselves.

The fitting heir to this Barthianism in not the old Barth, but his former fellow combatant, *Rudolf Bultmann,* with his existentialistic theology of 'demythologization', which has, during the last fifteen years of continental debate, somewhat stolen attention away from the old Barth (who is, as a matter of fact, two years younger than Bultmann).

At the same time Bultmann is carrying forth the inheritance from rationalism and liberalism; in contemporary theology the existentialistic school is advancing as the third 'modern' wave of attack on traditional Christianity. In the same way as its predecessors it is claiming restless respect for the outlook of 'modern man'. The mythological Biblical view of the universe must be replaced by the view of our own age. All the Biblical miracles and all the 'supernatural' elements of the creeds have to be given away. Only the Biblical interpretation of present human existence is a concern of ours.

The motivation behind this new theology is partly pedagogical: a radical transposition of the Gospel from a distant historical environment to the twentieth century is necessary, not only to avoid unnecessary offenses to human intellect but to make the point itself clear. But there is also a theological motivation which, to its spokesmen, seems quite important. They maintain that the new theology is a necessary consequence of the principle of 'justification by faith'. As soon as the church has a doctrine to present, a system of formulated truth, its champions are securing themselves by something that belongs to themselves. Faith as an unconditioned commitment to the grace of God in every shifting situation, has been changed into reliance upon general religious principles, through which we try to subjugate God. The doctrinal system, it is maintained, has thus become a new kind of self-justification — justification by works. A renewal of the reformatory revolution of faith has become necessary. But today this revolution can only take place through an existential approach to the problems.

## 2.

The dilemma of contemporary theology arises in the meeting between two parts with different and seemingly incompatible claims. Revelation claims to be taken seriously. So does the modern world. But is a co-existence possible without some kind of amputation that would render either Christianity or culture invalid?

There are in our time a great many people fairly interested in religion, whose spiritual nourishment consists in an unreflective humanism amalgamated with considerable remnants of rationalism and liberalism. They rejoice in a general praise of love and goodness and they honor Christ as a nice mascot, but reject the necessity of believing in those strange events of the past and in pronouncements about sin and grace and judgment. To them a real dilemma does not exist. They have placed themselves entirely beyond it.

So have many good Christians, to whom the Bible is, or at least is felt as, a familiar world, while modern thought and research is something very remote, insignificant and, perhaps, dangerous. In their view, arguing from the Scriptures against science is supporting the wisdom of God against the pride of this world. The Christian commits his thought to God in accepting every word of the Bible and every confessional statement of his church. Here too the dilemma is basically excluded.

As soon as Christianity and the world are both accepted as realities which have to be kept together, we stand in the midst of what I have called the dilemma. We stand between two claims which are both *just* claims. They seem to contradict each other. And those who have been trying to bring them together seem to have injured one or both of the claimants.

We have seen how and why the rationalist and the liberal approach had to fail. They omitted the very offense of the Gospel, and they made themselves servants of the favorite thoughts of their own era, and therefore the fate of their era became their fate also.

Today we are facing the challenge of Bultmannism and Tillichism and all the other specimens of theological existentialism. Can they help us? No doubt they have moved closer to the center of the conflict than did their predecessors. No doubt their efforts to render justice to both sides is more conscious, more purposeful and better motivated than were the rationalist and liberal enterprises. But is it possible to give away nearly all the historical facts referred to in our Creed, and to present Christianity as a nude event here and now? Is it true that the death and resurrection taking place when the Word is preaching new existence to me, are the real and only significance of the Death and resurrection of Christ? I cannot see that it should be.

The strongest argument of many existentialist theologians is this: The relation of a Christian to God must be a strictly personal face-to-face matter. Only the direct word of the living God forcing me anew and ever anew to depart from self-complacency and self-assurance, is my Christian concern. To make a doctrine out of this, to fence it in by general statements or to run away from it and concentrate attention on historical matters in the past or on interesting events in the future, means running into an illusion. Fleeing away from God, fleeing away from myself.

Therefore a true Christian theology should not occupy itself with the Biblical history or with dogmatic statements except as interpretations of present human existence. Only thus can it help man to discover the true meaning of justification by faith. For both historical and dogmatic theology are, if intending to provide some kind of substantial material as object for the act of belief, essentially attempts to obtain justification by works, by something we possess ourselves and over which we are able to exercise full control.

My main objection to this argumentation is this. No doubt dogmatics and creeds and confessions can be wrongly used as instruments for human pride and self-complacency: 'I am *completely right* in my assertion that all men are *completely wrong*'. But is it better to think like this: 'I have thrown all dogmatical conceptions away because I don't want to be among those proud and self-deceiving people who assure themselves by means of self-made performances'? Isn't even this ostentatious casting away of my own merits a new attempt to establish a merit? Imagine the customs official in the temple speaking: 'I thank Thee, my God, because I am not like this Pharisee who believes in his own virtues, his own community, his own dogmatics. I have thrown all those things away; I believe in nothing of my own. I am humble and my hands are empty, and blessed are the poor in Spirit . . .' Could, existentially speaking, a grosser lie be imagined than this?

When the Bultmannian school pretends to give better room to justification by faith alone, by its so-called demythologization, this pretension seems therefore to involve a basic illusion. By abandoning your dogmas you may of course also abandon a fleshly confidence in them, but most likely you will only have it changed into an even more fleshly confidence in your own non-dogmaticity.

Judged from its purely theological intentions, radical existentialist theology fails in its aim. I have had the opportunity to study this particularly in the works of the Danish church history professor and polemician *P. G. Lindhardt*. His books contain furious attacks on all present church groups because he finds them relying upon their own virtues. They feel sure in their own convictions, and this kind of assurance he judges to be the capital crime of which a Christian can make himself guilty. Well, in some sense he is right, but it is rather striking to read this in an author who himself displays an infinite assurance in his own right: 'I am completely sure that you are completely wrong, because you feel completely sure.'

In some sense every man has his dogmas. Even the assertion of being completely undogmatical is a dogma. Man is always tempted to find a false assurance in a Kingdom of his own, therefore also his thought and opinions and dogmas may easily become instruments of his self-deification — whatsoever these opinions may be. But, on the other hand, there are opinions or dogmas or messages that contain in themselves a perpetual warning. As long as you use a signboard for climbing on it does not matter whether the inscription is true or not. But as soon as you read it, it may be a matter of life and death. The Christian truth may also be used as a signboard for climbing on, and anyone who believes he is a true Christian by doing so is no better off than a man who uses any other signboard for the same purpose. But that does not prove that the inscriptions on signboards are useless in themselves. The approval of dogmas is no proof of a salutary faith, but the dogmas themselves may, in spite of this, be very reliable guides to this faith for anyone who really follows the road they are pointing out.

Many existentialists, even theologians, are subject to a very common error. They have seen a truth, and in their enthusiasm they proclaim that they have found *the* Truth. Their truth consists in a discovery of the poverty of man and the importance of doing away with all illusive comforts. We are all trying to hide behind each other; it is necessary to pull individual man out of the multitude, to make him be alone with himself, his own death, his own responsibility. And every means of escape must be taken away from him. Man, meet your own nothingness, see your own empty hands!

So far so good. Or, at least, almost so far. For this existentialist feeling of cosmic poverty is not exactly the same as a Christian experience of sin. What is the difference? The poor man of the Sermon on the Mount knows something decisive which the poor man of existentialism does not know: he knows the divine richness which he has rejected and feels his guilt for having rejected it. He knows too well that his own pitiable kingdom is a defiance of the kingdom of God that renders him guilty not only of self-deception but of God-desertion.

Here it becomes obvious that the average existentialist has seen only the half of human sin, and *that* half is not even the original one. He sees man running away from his individual self, and decides to chase him back. Very well. But *why* does man flee from this self? Isn't it because his self has become unbearable to him? Unbearable because he has broken that basic fellowship with his heavenly father and his earthly brothers which he was created for. The distress of Cain is not the disquietude and restlessness which force him to flee from himself, but the act that caused his distressful flight. It is the guilt, consciousness of which he is trying to escape.

To the Gospel, sin is something basically more than it is to existentialism; so also salvation from sin must be something more. Not only is it a return to my personal self, but also a return to the father and to the brothers I have forsaken. Most existentialists remain in a pointedly individualistic conception of ethics. They fear the neighbor because to them he means the temptation of flight, a possibility of seduction, a hindrance to a true experience of myself and my poverty. Even according to the Gospel I have to stop hiding myself behind the others, I have to come to myself. That is true, but it is not sufficient to go only so far. I have to return to my neighbor, and with a completely new purpose. Not to hide myself, but to reveal Christ. From the false fellowship where we all seek a cover against God, through individual unveiling and repentance, to a genuine fellowship under the Reign of God — that is the aim of Christianity.

This is the reason why Christian belief must attach such tremendous importance to the fact of the *Consummatum est.* There is something ready, there is something settled, before all our seeking and all our conversion. Sin and death have been vanquished, and a community of love and justice has been founded by an historical deed. God himself has incorporated his Son into fallen mankind. His suffering with us, and by us, is the supreme deed of communion which has once and for always opened to sinners the full community with God.

It is true that this must become real to me here and now, that the fellowship with the life, the death and the resurrection of Christ consists in something far more than mere historical knowledge of the facts, for his life, death and resurrection are events taking place in the life of every believer too. But the main point on which the attention of faith is fixed is not the reflections in the believer's own heart, but the historical deed which once took place independently of all my feelings and experiences. Only by first being an alien righteousness, a righteousness outside myself, a righteousness that is entirely the act of the God-Man, my Savior, can it become a personal experience embraced by faith.

In denying the unique historical event of Christ the incarnate God, namely by boiling down the fact to mere kerygmatic 'significance', some of the existentialist theological schools have clearly violated the basic interests of Christian faith. The existential approach to theology is in itself good and sound, and its Christian and Kierkegaardian sources are making their influence felt. The task of theology is not to find out everything between heaven and earth, but to trace a track; not to give answers to the questions of human curiosity, but to make the question of God heard and to point to him who reveals its answer. The origin of theological deliberation cannot be the question: who is God, what was his occupation before creation, how are heaven and hell constructed? Rather, it is simply this: what is his will of me; how has he presented himself to me in his Word (cf. Isa. lv:8-11)?

This means that a Christian theologian cannot read the Bible like the Mormons and the Watchtower Corporation do — to find out interesting things concerning future historical events and the geography of the transcendental world. The Bible is not an encyclopedia. Its center is he who is himself the 'Word', and every detail must be ranged according to its connection with him.

Therefore Christian faith can never feel bothered by the circumstance that there are many matters in the Bible which are

132

difficult to understand, and many verses that a sincere theologian knows can be subject only to a very uncertain exegesis. I think it was Mark Twain who once said: 'All the things I don't understand in Scriptures don't trouble me in the least compared to the things I do understand'. That seems to me to be a truly theological comment. If we know him who is the Lord and Master of the Book, and of ourselves, we may feel safe that it is all resting in his hand. The point is not to know the solutions of all riddles, but to know their Master.

This understanding must lead to freedom in facing the problem of the Bible and research. The absolute and radical uniqueness of Christ is a point I see no reason for discussing. Either I believe in him, or I do not believe. In the latter case, I should find no earnest reason for calling my standpoint Christianity. But at the same time I frankly confess, I do not believe in every statement contained in the Scriptures. Of course, in saying so, I have to explain what I mean by 'believe'. When I say that I believe in Christ, I do not mean the same thing as when I say I believe in the discovery of America by the Norwegian Viking Leif Eriksson. In the first case *believe* means committing myself with full confidence to a fact which reason cannot assure me of. In the second case it means judging what is probably true by means of rational deliberation, but without being existentially concerned with its truth. Even in the Bible there are many details in which I 'believe' in this second, not really religious, sense of the word.

In the Scriptures facts are contained which reveal Christ and which therefore are of real importance for my Christian life. And, on the other hand, there is much information which is in itself irrelevant in this basic connection. However, it is impossible for me, as for anyone, to draw a clear borderline between relevant and irrelevant matters in Scripture. There are things of which I certainly know to which side of the line they belong. The age of Methuselah is obviously unimportant for my salvation; the self-testimony of Christ is not. But between these matters there is a vast no man's land, where it is impossible to draw absolute conclusions. The frontiers of this no man's land may move a little from time to time, but in principle the no man's land will always be there. And this fact should not trouble us too much.

Faith has its dwelling-place at the Cross and at the broken grave of Christ. From this central point it constantly surveys the vast Biblical material and tries to bring new and deeper understanding of the central fact from the many more or less adjacent data. But, basically, 'belief' in the sense of 'faith' is a belief only in Christ. As to things I am not able to connect with this belief, they are not objects of faith at all. That doesn't mean, of course, that I believe that they are not true. I may, on entirely rational premises, be convinced of their truth. Take, for example, the travels of St. Paul: I believe in the survey given by the Acts, that is, my reason tells me that there is no reason to doubt the outline traced. But I don't *believe* it, not in the sense of putting my hope of salvation in it.

In stating this I have already suggested how the thought of a Christian moves forward from two different starting points, the starting points of faith and of reason. Reason is asking, What is probable? Faith is asking, What is revealing Christ? What, then, will happen if the very revelation of Christ should occur to reason as improbable? Then faith, with open eyes, will choose Christ and leave the considerations of probability at their worth. To a rational calculation, of course, an event like the resurrection of Christ is not 'probable'. But what does that really imply? Exactly this, that our experience informs us of thousands and thousands who have died and not returned to the number of living men, and of no one who has returned. From this seeming regularity we conclude a natural law: There exists no return from death. But as we all know, Peter or Paul would not have been shocked by our experience. What our reasoning contains is just this, that if a resurrection really has taken place, it must be unique, and our calculations leave no room for uniqueness. All our cognition operates through a practical assurance that coming events will happen according to a general pattern which we are familiar with from events that have already occurred. If we were deprived of this practical assurance, our world would be broken to pieces and we would stand quite helpless in an ever-changing chaos of surprise. But this general assurance forms no basis for categorical assertions. It does not exclude the possibility that in a particular situation new and hitherto unknown factors may come in and affect the outcome.

To a theoretical examination, its uniqueness renders the resurrection improbable. To a religious consideration, it is exactly this uniqueness that underlines its importance: if it had been possible for mortal man to vanquish death himself, the resurrection of Christ would be without basic importance. Thus exactly the same fact which renders it impossible for reason to affirm it, renders it necessary for faith to do so. If either part knows its limit, faith will not press reason to make invalid proofs, nor will reason force faith to abjure its belief.

I have tried to sketch how faith is dealing with the task of cognition. It remains to say something on reason and the Christian evaluation of thought. In the course of history reason has sometimes been regarded as the supreme religious faculty, and sometimes as the arch-foe of every sound subordination under divine authority. Which is true? Luther introduced a very good expression. He called reason 'the Devil's prostitute'. What is a prostitute? She is a creature that from the side of nature is as good as any, but is used for a purpose contrary to her true destiny. She has not been created by the Devil, she is just being abused by him. So also reason; it is a grant of God. The question is whether she is treated as a wife or as a prostitute.

The use of reason in religious matters is very necessary. It is necessary because my intellectual concepts will dethrone my religious conviction if this conviction is not able to express itself in concepts capable of disciplining them. It is dangerous because in questions where my personal existence is involved, reason is easily seduced by motives it has not taken time and trouble to make clear to itself. The French philosopher *Montaigne*, who was so strongly aware of this fact, points out two main seductive powers: desire and custom. Man, according to him, always chooses to do what is most convenient to his own flesh, and afterwards he will use his reason to prove for himself and others that only rational considerations have motivated his choice. First we act, then we call upon reason to justify our actions.

No doubt Montaigne has seen something rather important. How often we can see people simply searching for excuses when they compile arguments against Christianity! They use their reason to hide what are the real reasons for their standpoints.

A Christian has basically done away with his excuses, but even he will be tempted to find good and seemingly Christian reasons for his many smaller disobediences to God. Reason is always ready to undertake the defense when personal comfort needs it. What is bad is not the instrument, but the person who uses it, my own Ego. A spade is a good thing, and yet it may be used to put a man to death. A woman is also a good thing, and yet she may become a prostitute, if we may sustain Luther's analogy.

The perfection of reason consists in its capacity to find out its own limits. It can know the limited reach of its own general statements, and it can discover its dependence upon other, psychological powers. Reason itself is a neutral entity which registers and combines facts, indifferent to reluctance as well as to appreciation. But it is used by a personality who can never be neutral in questions which concern himself. Therefore my actual thought is always a mixed process, it consists not only of reasoning but is also mixed up with feeling, desires, conventions. I can register some of these non-intellectual influences upon my thought, but I can never get an exact and exhaustive concept of them all. So it becomes impossible for me to draw a sharp borderline even between the valid and invalid in my own thought. Facing my thought I stand in a situation that corresponds somewhat with the situation in which I stand when facing the Bible: as to details, there are a great many about which I may not be absolutely convinced. But the basic orientation, the starting points of my analysis, are clear. Reason itself is always in its right, but I am not always in my right in my use of it. Even the best and most useful instrument may be abused, used for wrong purposes, and the purposes of sinful man are always wrong.

To unveil the abuse of reason, reason itself can effectively contribute by discovering itself and its own instrumental status. And revelation will contribute through pointing out the decisive motives of sinful man and arresting his attempts at escape, and thus show how reason is not fostering unbelief, but is being used by unbelief as a cover.

It is my duty to stay suspicious, not against my reason, however, but against myself and my own use of reason for non-rational purposes. The same corrupt Old Adam who reads even Scriptures to find fig leaves that might cover his nudity and bushes that might conceal him so as to avoid the eye of the living God, persuades his reason not to examine its own status too closely, but to serve personal comfort and convenience with loyal obedience.

Thus thought has to be careful in whichever of the two directions it is moving. Starting from the presuppositions of mere reason it has to move forward slowly and carefully, consciously and constantly reminding itself to keep safely inside its limits. There are things it can affirm with what approximates to certainty, there are things it can conclude with different degrees of probability, and there are things which it must deliberately place outside its competence. Starting from the presuppositions of Christian faith, the situation will prove somewhat analogous. Also in its Biblical exegesis thought has to observe the commandments of caution; there are things which faith embraces as definitely true and decisive, there are things the historical truth or the religious importance of which are not perfectly clear, and there are things which can definitely be stamped unimportant. Space forces me to refrain from illuminating my statement by examples, but this might easily be done.

We have been speaking about the dilemma arising from the meeting between Revelation, given once and for all, and a temporal cultural pattern, our own time. Do the claims of faith and those of thought really contradict each other, or can they be reconciled? As you will understand from my sketch, I do not believe in a peace settlement that establishes all possible and impossible disputes for all time. But I definitely think that faith and reason, each inspecting and respecting its own essential quality, may find a mode of co-existence that violates neither of the two. They have to admit that they are not omniscient, they have to discern between what they know and what they don't know, and, not least, they have to know why they want to know in order to make out which questions are their concern and which not.

Some audacious and polemical churchmen in the course of history have liked to talk of belief 'against' reason. No, said the Roman church, belief is not against but 'above' reason. They are both right and they are both wrong. Christianity is not against reason in itself, but it is definitely against Old Adam using reason; and therefore I can never use my own reasoning as a standard of my religious cognition. That belief is above reason is also right: reason is right as far as it can reach and no farther — but again we have to add: its deficiency consists not only in shortcomings, the *against* must be remembered too. Christianity is *above* reason and *against* man who is constantly abusing reason. But there is another side of the matter too: Christianity and reason work *together* in unveiling their mutual relationship, and it is possible for them to agree upon a conclusion.

How can such a conclusion be worked out today? No doubt there is much prejudice to be vanquished in the minds of so-called 'modern' men. The superstitious cult of science and reason has been losing ground among the real scholars in the twentieth century, but in revenge it has been winning many proselytes among the ordinary newspaper-informed layers of western society, even among people with considerable religious sympathies. A realistic modesty in the evaluation of reason and research is necessary. The average 'modern' mind of today should not be allowed to dictate to the Church the conditions of an armistice.

On the other hand, the ordinary Christian outlook, which, for better or for worse, differs from that of advanced modern theologians, may also be ripe for a comprehensive reformation — not to be driven from its own Scylla to the Charybdis of the theologians mentioned, but to be led into a safe passage somewhere in the middle. When belief in Christ is affirmed as the invariable basis of theological thought, this thought itself must be free to form new opinions on details after it has evaluated the conclusions of historical and scientific research. When asked by my students at the Teacher's training college at Oslo about how to read the Bible, I used to say: 'There are matters in the Bible which were easy to accept in its own time, but which for us are hard to accept — those are the matters connected with variable customs and opinions, and they are not decisive for our faith. On the other hand there are the matters which were just as difficult for men then as they are for us now. These are matters revealing the invariable relationship between God and man, and they are decisive.' God's absolute claim of sovereignty, God's absolute gift of grace — these two points must by all means be kept in mind and underlined. But the seven days of creation, the age of the patriarchs, or the whale of Jonah — I cannot see how our salvation should be affected if they were dispensed with as literal historical facts.

The starting point of modern existential theology seems to me to be all right and to be basically consistent with the starting point of St. Paul and of Martin Luther: what we need is to know the track we are on, not the particular details of far-off landscapes in different directions. But a closer contact is needed with the Bible than with the professors Bultmann and Tillich — the Bible, not as a religious Encyclopedia, but as a testimony to Christ and his historical deed of Reconciliation.

Even the doctrine of verbal inspiration may be said to contain a not unimportant element of truth. The different Biblical books are something far more than what their authors understood and planned. The full Bible, which none of its authors ever knew they were contributing to, was planned and produced by the Holy Spirit. Not, however, in the sense that every detail should, itself, be received as a divine oracle, but in the sense that the totality of Scripture given to us is a message from God, to which the authors have contributed far beyond what they personally understood. Our time has to break the bounds of historical exegesis and march back to truly theological exegesis. We must proceed from the question, What does the author intend to say? — although this may be significant enough — to another question, What does God intend to say? And this question can only be answered when the single verse or chapter or book is considered within the fullness of the Scriptures, that is, when interpreted *to* and *in* and *by* Christ, the Word himself.

During this essay I have left more questions unanswered than answered, and more problems unproposed than proposed. I am sure that most of my readers have a feeling of having been roving in vast woods in the company of a guide who has not been too eager to bring them safely through. That is true. What theology has to seek is not a deliverance from all problems, but a basic clarity which makes it possible to exist in the problems without losing confidence and courage. A faith which has seen the living Christ and a reason which has seen its own limits hold a basic clarity which cannot be obscured by the many single questions yet unsolved. And their co-existence is not a state merely of passive toleration but of promissory collaboration.